Woodbrooke College

200 11256

THE COSMOS
AND THE CREATOR

An Introduction to the
Theology of Creation

DAVID A. S. FERGUSSON

First published in Great Britain 1998
Society for Promoting Christian Knowledge
Holy Trinity Church
Marylebone Road
London N W I 4D U

Copyright © David A. S. Fergusson 1998

All rights reserved. No part of this book may be
reproduced or transmitted in any form or by any means,
electronic or mechanical, including photocopying,
recording, or by any information storage and
retrieval system, without permission in
writing from the publisher.

Scripture quotations are from
The New Revised Standard Version of the Bible © 1989.

British Library Cataloguing-in-Publication Data
A catalogue record of this book is available from
the British Library

ISBN 0–281–05068–6

Typeset by Wilmaset Ltd, Birkenhead, Wirral
Printed in Great Britain by
Arrowsmiths Ltd, Bristol

To Margot

Contents

Preface

The material which forms this short study was first presented at a course of Sunday evening studies in 1994 at a conjoint gathering of the congregations of Holburn West Church and Queen's Cross Church, Aberdeen. I am grateful to Bob Brown and Mike Mair for their invitation to participate in this series, and to all those who took part. The hymn, 'We thank you God for what we are' was composed by Mike Mair for a closing act of worship. Since it seemed to express the doxological significance of our theme much better than anything I said, it is included with his permission.

The chapters of this book represent a revised version of four Cunningham Lectures delivered at New College, University of Edinburgh, in July 1996. I am grateful to the Principal and Senate of New College, and to the Dean and Faculty of Divinity for their generous invitation to present these lectures during the 150th anniversary celebrations at New College, my alma mater. I am also glad to record a debt of gratitude to the many friends, including former teachers, colleagues and students, who attended the lectures, and who offered such constructive comment during the times set aside for discussion. The final writing-up of the material has been completed during a period of study leave at the Center of Theological Inquiry, Princeton. I am indebted to Niels Gregersen of Aarhaus University for his helpful comments on a draft of Chapter Three during our time together in Princeton.

David A. S. Fergusson

'We thank you God for what we are'
(Tune: Tallis Canon)

We thank you God for what we are;
As bodies formed from space and star;
As minds which grew from beast and flower;
As spirits sharing in your power.

We thank you God for our unique
Capacity to think and speak;
To name the world and understand
What your designing love has planned.

We thank you God that we are free
To choose what we shall do and be;
And when we've chosen dark and loss
We find you waiting on a cross.

We thank you God that we can hope
Our lives may match your wisdom's scope;
That through the agonies of earth
Your spirit gives your children birth.

We thank you God for what you are
As fashioner of space and star;
As Christ of laughter and of pain;
As Spirit mothering again.

M. V. A. Mair

==

CHAPTER ONE

Creation in the Bible

Introduction

At first glance creation looks the least problematic of the doctrines of the Christian faith. It is set out at the beginning of the Bible. Parents and teachers can present it to young children as a way of characterizing God. It makes sense not only to Christians but also to Jews and Muslims who share in some measure the doctrine of creation out of nothing. Even outwith these religious communities there are many who still assent to the idea of creation as making sense of the existence and order of the cosmos.

The doctrine of creation has not been at the centre of any of the great theological controversies of the history of the Church. It does not appear to divide the various traditions within the Church. Unlike grace, the Trinity, the person of Christ, the sacraments, and predestination, the doctrine of creation has been the cause neither of Christian division nor of the anathematizing of heretics. The Orthodox, Roman Catholic, Lutheran, Anglican and Reformed Churches can all affirm the ancient doctrine of the creation of the world by God out of nothing.

For much of the twentieth century, creation has been off the theological agenda. It was the doctrines of sin, grace and revelation which figured in the dialectical theologians' response to late-nineteenth- and early-twentieth-century liberalism. The shadow that Karl Barth cast over natural theology perhaps intimidated many Protestant theologians from venturing into the territory of the theology of creation. Ironically, it was Barth himself who produced the most substantial doctrine of creation in the third volume of the *Church Dogmatics*, after some of his critics said that he could not do it. Similarly, in biblical studies Gerhard von Rad's (early) preoccupation with salvation history seemed to relegate creation to the status of a by-product of Old Testament theology. The search for the distinctiveness of Old Testament religion lay not in its belief in creation but in its conviction of divine revelation in history. Moreover, it has been pointed out that, as recently as the 1970s, Hans Küng, a Roman Catholic theologian, could write over 700 pages *On Being a Christian* without the index carrying a single reference to the subject of creation.

Now this has all changed. The need to position Christianity in relation to the other religions, most notably Judaism and Islam, has brought about a renewed attention to the theme of creation. A-level students in Religious Studies are exposed to the Kalam cosmological argument for the existence of God. Environmentalists have raised hard questions about the friendliness of the Judaeo-Christian tradition to ecological responsibility. The World Council of Churches' project on 'Justice, Peace and the Integrity of Creation' has drawn attention to historical formulations of the doctrine of creation as has the recent evangelical declaration on Christian responsibility for the world. Increasingly militant concern for animal welfare has raised acute questions about theological attitudes to non-human creatures.

Modern science, moreover, has thrown up a number of issues requiring theological reflection. Cosmologists write books almost every month, it seems, arguing that the form and content of the physical universe display an elegance and delicate balance which suggest that is has an intelligent creator. Recent literature has speculated on the eventual destiny of life within a cosmos which will not survive indefinitely in its present form. You can buy in every Dillons and Waterstones in the UK books on the first three minutes and last three minutes of the universe. More hostile biologists point to the randomness of the evolutionary process. They ask, for instance, why God created dinosaurs, and whether the bloody and pitiless struggle of species to survive is really the mark of a well-designed universe.

Feminists and process theologians have also registered concerns about the way in which the traditional doctrine of creation characterizes the God–world relation. It construes God as apart from and transcendent to the creation. It reinforces notions of the sovereignty of God which are inimical to the need for mutuality, love, connectedness and wholeness. There thus emerges a more thoroughly immanentist understanding of the God–world relation which in some respects revives ancient pagan notions of the eternity of creation. This movement towards immanentism is related to a wider cultural movement in which the divine is seen as embedded within the created order. The holism of the New Age and its resonance with Eastern patterns of thought seem to offer something radically different from the Judaeo-Christian understanding of creation.

If hitherto the doctrine of creation has been an uncontested theological item, it has now become the territory on which rival theologies join battle. My argument throughout this brief study will be that the doctrine of creation must remain a distinctively Christian article of faith. However, it must also recognize and accommodate some of the criticisms that have been laid at the door of its traditional formulations together with the best insights from other disciplines. This is a desideratum for Christian theology in every area of study.

Creation in the Old Testament

In his early work, Gerhard von Rad tends to ascribe to the creation theology of Israel a subordinate role to the account of salvation history. When the Old Testament speaks of creation it does so generally in relation to Yahweh's saving action in history. 'Israel looked back in faith from her own election to the creation of the world, and from there drew the line to herself from the outermost limit of the protological to the center of the soteriological.'[1] The older creation traditions, probably derived from Canaanite sources, are perceived as incidental, whereas the creation theology of the wisdom literature is superimposed upon a tradition in which belief in salvation history has already become axiomatic. Creation theology is more like a by-product than a necessary ingredient of Hebrew faith. It was partly through this underestimate of the significance of creation in the Old Testament that it received relatively little attention earlier this century.

More recent scholarship, however, has questioned whether the creation theology of the Old Testament can be assigned this subordinate status.[2] What we have is more like two distinct expressions of faith which the canon struggles to integrate. This tension experienced within the Old Testament raises issues for subsequent theology. Any attempt to view creation theology as a by-product of redemption theology must reckon with the observation that all the cultures of the ancient Near East dealt extensively with creation in their myths and rituals. The preoccupation with creation was not primarily a desire to explain the origin of the world and the source of life. The order of the world required to be renewed year by year. Human life depended upon the divine maintenance of this cosmic harmony. This order, moreover, extended to human affairs. According to the royal Psalms, the order of the original creation is mediated through the king to his people. The king, like God, whose rule he reflects, maintains order by administering justice and defeating the enemies of the nation. Social justice and prosperity are thus features of a single cosmic harmony under the rule of God. 'Law, nature and politics are only aspects of one comprehensive order of creation.'[3] The security of the state, its observance of a legal code, and its social and economic prosperity are all part of a single created order which must be respected, cherished and maintained. 'Let the heavens be glad, and let the earth rejoice ... for he is coming to judge the earth. He will judge the world with righteousness, and the peoples with his truth' (Ps. 89.9–11, 19).

Scholarship in the history of religions has shown that stories of creation are found throughout the world in the oldest cultures. Myths of creation have the function not only of depicting the origin of the world, but also of ensuring through recital and enactment the maintenance of natural and social harmony. We need creation stories to find our place in the world, to find roots by which we can understand who we are and where we have come from. Thus R. Pettazoni in his work on the social anthropological function of creation myths writes. 'The proper worth of myth consists in the necessary and sufficient justification which it gives to whatever is most essential to human life and to society, by relating it to a primordial act of foundation recorded by the myth. ... The recital of the myth of the origins of the world makes real and guarantees the stability and duration of the universe.'[4]

Neither the universality nor the similarity of creation myths should trouble Christian theology. We should resist the temptation to search frantically for distinctive elements within the ancient Hebrew account of creation. Distinctiveness will inevitably emerge through patient exposition since in most religions one article of faith is conditioned by all the others. In this respect, the biblical account of creation will take care of its own distinctiveness as it becomes integrated with other biblical themes. In any case, where the Church's doctrine of creation shares similarities with other traditions, or shows evidence of borrowing from outwith, we can acknowledge that the fundamental questions about God and human existence are not confined to any one province of the created order.

The theme of cosmic order is already present in Israelite life in the time of the early monarchy. Yahweh made a covenant with David and chose Jerusalem as the divine dwelling-place.[5] Psalm 89 is silent about the exodus tradition but celebrates the enthronement of David (cf. 2 Sam. 7) alongside the creation of the world from out of chaos. 'You rule the raging of the sea; when its waves rise you still them. You crushed Rahab like a carcass; you scattered your enemies with your mighty arm ... Then you spoke in a vision to your faithful one, and said: "I have set the crown on one who is mighty, I have exalted one chosen from the people. I have found my servant David; with my holy oil I have anointed him"' (Ps. 89.10, 11, 19).

It can be argued that the context of the Near-Eastern view of the order of creation is the setting for much that is found in the prophetic literature. In this respect the story of salvation history becomes intertwined with the story of the cosmos. Jeremiah perceives that God's rule over history is underscored by God's identity as the creator. 'Ah Lord God! It is you who made the heavens and the earth by your great power and by your outstretched arm! Nothing is too hard for you' (Jer. 32.17).

Apart perhaps from the opening chapters of the Bible,

creation theology finds its most profound expression in the exilic writings of Second Isaiah. The greatness and incomparability of Yahweh are shown both in the leading of Israel through the Red Sea, and in the creation of the world. Creation and salvation are thus integrated. It is not merely that creation as an ancillary theme becomes bolted on to a preconceived theology of salvation history. The vision of a new future is one that is shaped by creation motifs. Yahweh's power and grace embrace not only Israel but all the nations. The hope of Israel thus extends to other peoples and even to the non-human creation. This is developed in Third Isaiah with its picture of a transfigured creation. 'The wolf and the lamb shall feed together, the lion shall eat straw like the ox: but the serpent – its food shall be dust!' (Isa. 65.25).

This poetic description of the transfiguration of both nature and history is curiously modern in at least two respects. The cosmos, as we now know it through modern science, is not a static arena in which the drama of human history is played out. The universe has its own history from the big bang to either a big crunch or a final burn out. It has undergone some dramatic changes in the course of that history and may be expected to undergo many more. We ourselves are part of a larger history. Our human story is situated within the narrative of creation. Our identity and destiny cannot be understood apart from that of the cosmos. In this respect, the integration of nature and human history in a redeemed world is a necessary feature of any modern eschatology. Morevoer, the location of human redemption in a wider cosmic framework may caution against an exclusive humanocentrism in theology. The world was not made for human beings only. Other creatures have their place in God's creation and final purpose. This point was well made by Angela Tilby in her TV Series *The Soul*.

[R]ather than seeing the universe as the background for the human adventure, we should see ourselves as part of its adventure. The whole cosmos is the adventure and our human journey is a part of that, rather than it being merely a part of ours. The double effect of this is that we are brought back into the processes of the universe, and yet at the same time are humbled by a new recognition of our limitations. We belong, but we are not all there is. We are here, but it was not made just for us.[6]

Although there is a wealth of reference to creation in the Psalms and prophetic literature, it is the opening chapters of Genesis which have dominated Judaeo-Christian approaches to the doctrine of creation. Claus Westermann in his typology of creation myths distinguishes four broad types found in the religious traditions of the world. These are creation by birth, creation as the result of a struggle or victory, creation by divine act, and creation through the word.[7] In the opening chapter of Genesis there is little trace of either the first or the second, creation by birth or creation through struggle.

Despite its context within ancient Near-Eastern traditions, the Genesis account reveals some striking differences. In the Sumerian mythology, the world comes into being through a succession of births, including the birth of the gods. For the Old Testament, however, no intermediary gods are required to bring about the creation of the world. The nearest we come to this idea is in the idea of the agency of wisdom. Yet although Arius was later to exploit Proverbs 8.22 – the Lord created me at the beginning of his work – it seems clear that wisdom is better thought of as a predicate of God rather than a second god who has been created for the sake of creating the world.

Creation as a result of a struggle or victory is the dominant theme in the Babylonian creation myth in which Marduk creates the world out of the body of the sea-monster, Tiamat, whom he has slain. There are hints of this theme in Isaiah 27, Psalm 74 and Job 26 and also in Genesis 1.2 with its reference to the formless void and the darkness over the face of the deep. Here the presence of a primeval chaos seems to precede and menace the creative activity of God. Yet these echoes of struggle notwithstanding, creation in Genesis is largely an effortless activity which reflects the power of God over what has been called into being.

The sharp distinction between creator and creation in the Old

Testament entails that greater prominence is given in Genesis 1 to the notions of creation as an act and creation through the word. Creation takes place through an act of separation in Genesis 1, the separation of light from darkness and land from sea. This is closely related to creation through the word of God. These acts of separation follow upon the command that this should take place. Similar motifs are found in Psalm 33.9 and Isaiah 48.13. Creation, as one commentator puts it, takes place through a series of word-fulfilment events in which there is a stylistic connection between command and execution.[8] This is apparent also in the flood story at Genesis 6.22. The independence and sovereignty of God are embedded in this narrative. There is no struggle that takes place. God is not identified with any of the forces at work in nature. There is no divinizing of the earth, the sky or the sun. The supreme personal initiative of God in creating the heavens and the earth is later paralleled by the covenants that God brings about with Noah, and with Abraham and his descendants.

Brevard Childs in his recent *Biblical Theology of the Old and New Testaments* remarks that the Israelite world view is one which draws a sharp distinction between God and the creation. The material world as freely created is purged of divine and demonic elements. Thus the Psalmist can claim that the heavens announce the glory of God but 'there is no speech, nor are there words; their voice is not heard' (Ps. 19.3).[9] Childs argues that this stress upon the transcendence of God and the otherness of the world places a question mark against any form of panentheism, the fashionable doctrine that God's being is entirely immanent in the world. Criticism of monarchial models of God has led many theologians to insist upon God's total indwelling of the world. This, however, neglects the ontological distinction which is central to the scriptural differentiation of God and the world, and to its perception of the way in which God interacts with the creation. Much is at stake in this distinction, and much is lost if it is abolished in favour of an alternative construction of the God–world relation. I shall argue later that it is for this reason that recent eco-feminist theology is fixed on a post-Christian trajectory.[10]

It is clear that we have two creation stories in Genesis with different emphases which have been united in the final form of the canon. Old Testament scholarship has, for the most part, assigned these to the P and J strands within the Pentateuch, i.e. to the Priestly and Jahwistic writers. The distinctive styles are characterized in the following way in a recent popular commentary. 'J is marked by lively anthropomorphisms, vivid storytelling, and creative theological vision (promise/fulfilment dynamic). J articulated the old traditions, perhaps in response to Solomonic enlightenment. ... P is another clearly marked strand. It is concerned with questions of cult and ritual (Lev), is interested in genealogies (Gen), and in contrast to the "Name" theology of Deut speaks of the presence of God in terms of glory and tabernacling (Ex. 16.10; 40.34–8).'[11]

The J account is thought to have originated around 1000 BC in the time of Solomon, whereas the P account may have originated in the time of the exile in Babylon around 550 BC. To attempt to date and trace the development of these traditions within the canon is a complex if not impossible task. Although these issues are not unimportant they may be regarded as of secondary significance in the present context, since, from a theological perspective, we have to enquire as to the function of the narratives within the canon as a whole.[12]

There is certainly no shortage of interesting questions that a modern reader brings to these texts. The most obvious of these concerns the six days of creation. This was the cause of much ecclesiastical strife in the nineteenth century. A clear sign of this perplexity in Scotland was the 1879 Declaratory Act of the United Presbyterian Synod, which in its final paragraph stated that in holding to the Westminster Confession of Faith 'liberty of opinion is allowed on such points ... not entering into the substance of the faith, as the interpretation of the "six days" in the Mosaic account of the creation'. The six days of creation and Archbishop Ussher's dating of the universe to 4004 BC had, since the late eighteenth century, been found problematic. The geological work of scholars like Charles Lyell suggested that the world must be much older and that it had reached its present form through long processes of gradual transformation.

To accommodate these insights within Christian theology, the popular writer Hugh Miller had suggested that the 'days' of Genesis were long intervals of indefinite length.[13]

It would be wrong, however, to assume that a literalistic reading of the six days dominated the Christian tradition in earlier times. On the contrary, this might even be seen as a modern aberration. The theologians of the early Church were a good deal more sophisticated than is often recognized. The nature of the firmament and its place at the beginning of the creation story troubled exegetes. Could there be a sky on the day before there was an earth? The six days of creation could hardly be understood literally since it is asserted that day and night existed before the sun and the earth were made. The light, moreover, which is created on the first day cannot be the light of the sun which came into being on the fourth day. Accordingly, Augustine regarded this light as the spiritual light of heaven, a light which surrounded angelic beings. At the opening of Genesis the heaven is the eternal spiritual 'heaven of heaven' and the earth is formless matter lacking order or any process of temporal succession. This initial creation of heaven and earth, argued Augustine, precedes the first day and must be regarded as non-temporal.[14] The 'days' of creation refer to unknown periods of time. 'What kind of days these are is difficult or even impossible for us to imagine, to say nothing of describing them.'[15]

Scientific difficulties notwithstanding, a straight literalistic reading of the Genesis narratives is already rendered inappropriate by the canonical juxtaposition of two different accounts of creation with their different emphases and themes, by the mythological elements in the stories (particularly J), and by the adaptation of materials that feature in other ancient Near-Eastern cultures. The religious proclamation of the writer(s) is couched in terms of a highly primitive cosmology, and we should not try to save the former by attempting to square the latter with modern science. This needs to be made clear at the outset in the way in which Genesis 1 is taught at school and Sunday School.

Russell Stannard in his recent Radio 4 Series *Science and Wonders* laments the way in which children in their teens grow out of earlier religious convictions. One of the primary causes of this is that the science they learn in physics and biology classes appears to contradict the stories they were taught in primary school about God's creating the world.

> It is commonly held that religion is something you grow out of; that when it comes to the big questions of life – those to do with meaning and purpose, and where we humans fit into the overall picture – we should be looking not to religion, as was done in the past, but to science. Though people still retain a sense of awe and wonder when confronted by the mysteries of the universe, the sense of worship to which this sometimes leads has been displaced from God to science.[16]

It is for this reason that the Scottish Office syllabus for RE in our primary schools has got it right. It insists that children should be taught from Primary 5 onwards that the biblical creation story need not be believed in a literal sense. 'A useful approach at this stage would simply be to show how the story relates to human questions about how and why the world began. The rhythmic, poetic effect of Genesis chapter 1 can be brought out as can the lessons to be learnt about human nature from the Adam and Eve story.'[17]

What is perhaps regrettable about our current educational scene is that the passages of the Bible known best to children are the opening sequences of both the testaments, the creation story in the Old and the Christmas story in the New. A failure to relate these opening scenes to what comes later leads to a loss of connection with the ongoing activity of God in the history of the covenant. For the Old Testament the doctrine of creation is not merely an account of how the world got going. It is the first episode in a history. It points forward to God's further initiatives in his dealings with Noah, Abraham and Moses. Childs makes the point that the canonical shape of Genesis 1—2 directs us to humankind and its history. Chapter 2 has the function of beginning the story of Adam and Eve which succeeds the creation of the heavens and the earth.[18]

Creation as an initial act and continuous creation are comple-

mentary themes for Scripture. Continuous creation can be em-
phasized as arising out of rather than replacing the initial act of
creation. Creation is ongoing in that the initial act already has a
goal which is not yet achieved. Creation has the character of
becoming from the outset.[19] The continuing activity of God,
moreover, extends to nature as well as history. There is both an
original act of creation and a perpetual preservation of the
cosmos. God maintains creation within the orders that he has
created. This is the special theme of the Noahic covenant, and
is signified by the rainbow. The alternation of day and night,
and the sequence of the seasons manifest the order that God
maintains (Pss. 74.16f.; 136.8). It also involves God's caring for
each individual creature, providing it with food and water
(Deut. 11.12–15; Jer. 5.24; Pss. 104.13f.; 145.15f.). 'When you
send forth your spirit, they are created; and you renew the face
of the ground' (Ps. 104.30).[20]

Commentators argue about the meaning of the opening
phrase of the Bible. A difficulty arises over the meaning of the
very first phrase *bereshith*. It is an expression that by grammatical
convention should govern an event or an object so that it
denotes the beginning of something. In this grammatical
context, the traditional Jewish and Christian translation 'in the
beginning' seems anomalous. This problem is reflected in the
different renderings offered by the NRSV translation of the
English Bible. Three alternatives are presented. These are: in
the beginning when God created; when God began to create;
in the beginning God created. Much depends on how one
judges the context. The fact that the creation of the heavens is
not further mentioned might suggest that the traditional translation is correct. It is a majestic summary statement of what God
has done. Yet this need not detain us, for theologically it makes
little difference. However we construe the Hebrew, we do not
have here in Genesis 1.1 an explicit statement of creation out of
nothing. The reason for this is that the earth as a formless void
could not be the result of a creative act of God. Order is the
effect of God's word. The formless void is the antithesis of
order, and must be thought in some sense to pre-exist the
original act of creation. The *tohu wabohu* is an expression that else-

where in the Old Testament denotes the desert or the wilderness (cf. Isa. 34.11 and Jer. 4.23). It contrasts with the order of creation. Jewish and early Christian theologians did not understand Genesis 1.1 as implying creation out of nothing, since many regarded this verse as entirely compatible with Plato's account in the *Timaeus* of creation out of pre-existent matter. In the Middle Ages the Jewish theologian Gersonides would ask pointedly 'what about the waters?' Where did this surd element in creation come from if it was already there when God created the heavens and the earth?

The Image of God and the Problem of Dominion

A further issue of contested interpretation in the tradition concerns what it means to be created in the image of God (Gen. 1.26–7). Careful exegesis of the expressions for the image and likeness of God in the context of the Old Testament reveal that this cannot be identified with the possession of an immortal soul or mind. For Philo, the word 'image' is taken to refer to the mind which rules the body. The human mind is related to the body in an analogous manner to the relationship of the divine mind to the world. This analogical similarity creates a desire within the human mind for a return to the divine.[21] Such a reading of the text, however, betrays the distorting influence of Platonism.

Despite its prominence in Christian anthropology, the Old Testament speaks very sparingly about human beings as created in the image of God. One might argue indeed that the opening three chapters of the Bible have exercised an undue influence on the Church's theological traditions at the expense of other themes within the canon. Doubtless, the spare reference to the *imago Dei* has something to do with the prohibition on graven images or idols in the Decalogue (Exod. 20.4; Deut. 5.8, where the term *temunah* is used). The Hebrew *ṣelem* which appears in Genesis 1.26 should be rendered in a stronger physicalist sense than the Platonic reading of Philo suggests. Elsewhere the Hebrew word refers to something concrete and visible, e.g. a picture drawn on a wall (Ezek. 23.14) or a statue of a god (2

Kings 11.18; Dan. 3.1). Even if the further reference to 'likeness' (*demuth*) moves in the direction of greater abstraction,[22] one cannot avoid the holism of Hebrew anthropology. As a psychosomatic being *adam* images God by responding to God's initiative and by acting *in loco Dei*. Gerhard von Rad writes, 'Just as powerful earthly kings, to indicate their claim to dominion, erect an image of themselves in the provinces of their empire where they do not personally appear, so man is placed upon earth in God's image as God's sovereign emblem.'[23] The function of the human being is to exercise God's rule over the non-human creation. Genesis 1.26–7 seems to be glossed by Psalm 8.3, a rare development of this theme in the Old Testament. 'What are human beings that you are mindful of them, mortals that you care for them? Yet you have made them a little lower than God, and crowned them with glory and honour. You have given them dominion over the works of your hands: you have put all things under their feet.' The high status given to us is reflected in our dominion over God's handiwork. The image of God is thus to be understood not substantively in terms of the possession of an immortal soul, but relationally in terms of the role that human beings play before God and before the rest of creation.

Yet this attempted construction of the *imago Dei* only gives rise to another problem. Is the dominion granted to human beings over the creation ecologically objectionable? Do we have here the source of Lynn White's accusation in his seminal article of 1967 that the Judaeo-Christian tradition has licensed exploitative and supremacist attitudes towards the created order.[24] On reading today von Rad's comment that Adam is 'really only God's representative, summoned to maintain and enforce God's claim to dominion over the earth' one is instinctively uneasy.[25]

A standard response amongst the commentators is to argue that dominion is to be understood not as aggressive exploitation but as responsible stewardship. Thus Bernhard Anderson claims that

> the special status of humankind as the image of God is a call to re-
> sponsibility, not only in relation to other humans but also in

relation to nature. Human dominion is not to be exercised wantonly but wisely and benevolently so that it may be, in some degree, the sign of God's rule over the creation. Some of Israel's laws place restrictions on the careless harming and spoiling of nature, for instance the law prohibiting the taking of a mother bird (Deut. 22.6), or the command not to muzzle an ox while it treads the grain (Deut. 25.4) or the concern for trees (Deut. 20.19–20).[26]

We can thus interpret dominion in terms of a benign stewardship which emphasizes the relational rather than the substantive sense of the *imago Dei*. The unique role given to human beings is to be understood in terms of a relationship to care for and to preserve the creation. Their relationship with God brings obligations to act faithfully and responsibly within the world, and to offer up creation's praise to its Maker.[27] One might also add that the christological constructions of divine power and the notion of Christ as the bearer of the *imago Dei* also lead in this direction. Power is to be exercised only through self-sacrificial love. There thus lies at the centre of the Christian gospel a criticism of exploitative models of power, and a way of recasting earlier notions of dominion.[28] It has also been claimed that the Hebrew verb *radah* – translated 'to have dominion over' – in Genesis 1.28 has the basic sense of 'to wander around'. Its semantic field includes 'accompany', 'pasture', 'guide', 'lead', 'rule' and 'command'. The meaning of dominion therefore has to be understood, at least in this passage, in the context of shepherding.[29] Human beings are to rule the creation in the sense of being its shepherds, a much more benign and eco-friendly notion than the dominion of a ruthless tyrant.

It has been argued by some scholars that it is significant that in Genesis 1.26–30 humankind is not given permission to eat meat.[30] This is conceded only after the flood in Genesis 9.3–4. The ideal is vegetarian. No force will be exercised over the animal creation. Only after the flood is there a compromise. This reading of portions of Genesis 1—11 anchors these texts firmly in the situation of post-exilic Israel. Genesis 1 becomes a prophetic text, depicting an ideal of human society, a redeemed

creation marked by harmony between the species. It thus reso-
nates with other prophetic passages such as Isaiah 65.17–25,
which looks forward to a new age of health and natural prosperity in which even the animals no longer prey upon one another.
'The wolf and the lamb shall feed together, the lion shall eat
straw like the ox: but the serpent – its food shall be dust! They
shall not hurt or destroy on all my holy mountain, says the Lord.'

This of course may be only one strand within the canon. But
even if this is a minority view suppressed by an otherwise carni-
vorous canon, God's care of nature (and hence of human
responsibility for it) is a recurrent feature. The Genesis 2 narrative speaks of Adam as a caretaker of God's good garden. The
covenant with Noah, signified by the rainbow in the sky,
embraces 'every living creature of all flesh' (Gen. 9.8–17).

The difficulty with the notion of stewardship is that it remains
for some commentators too humanocentric. To depict the relationship of human beings as like a shepherd to a flock or a
manager to a set of resources is to present the rest of creation as
somehow given to us for our benefit. At any rate, the model of
stewardship carries that risk. It can too easily suggest that the
creation is made for us and for our benefit. Thus we have the
modern heresy of humanocentrism or anthropocentrism. As
Ruth Page has argued

> [t]he contemporary importance of stewardship cannot be
> doubted, for we have to manage our way out of the mess. But
> in theology that emphasis needs to be complemented by one
> which celebrates the independence of the natural world from
> humanity under God, and expresses a fellow-feeling (rather
> than a management-feeling) for our fellow creatures, since we
> are all part of the one creation.[31]

There are, however, resources in Scripture and tradition for re-
cognizing this. It would be wrong to assume that the world
was made solely for us. Psalm 104 speaks of Yahweh having
made all his creatures and taking delight in all his manifold
works. Job 39—41 speaks of God's taking delight in creatures
which have no apparent usefulness. The creation story of

Genesis 1 records that at each stage of creation God saw that it was good. The goodness of created things resides not in some instrumental value that they have for human use. Their goodness lies both in what they are of themselves and in their place in the overall harmony of creation. Gerard Manley Hopkins sought to express the value of created things by use of the concept of 'inscape'. This word occurs nearly fifty times in the journal which he kept from 1868 to 1875.[32] The term is applied to some particular thing of beauty which is distinctive and patterned. Inscape is used variously, but it applied both to the individuality and distinctiveness of created things and also to their configuration and design, their contribution to some wider purpose. The expression of inscape was in his poetry what melody was in music and design in painting. For Hopkins as poet and priest, the beauty of the world bears witness to the beauty of God displayed in Christ. As a young novice he could write, 'I do not think I have ever seen anything more beautiful than the bluebell I have been looking at. I know the beauty of our Lord by it. Its inscape is mixed of strength and grace.' The theology of his poetry enabled him to see both the indwelling of God in all things and also their witness to Christ as the one through whom and for whom all things were made.

We might also recognize the further feature of Genesis 1 that the crowning moment of creation is not the creation of Adam and Eve but the sabbath day of rest on which the whole creation glorifies its maker. On the first sabbath God looks back upon the goodness of creation, but the sabbath is also a sign of the future for the Old Testament. It points forward in anticipation of the Jubilee year of freedom and restoration (Lev. 25.8–55). There will be a 'sabbath without end' (Jub. 2.19–24). Walter Brueggemann writes

Sabbath is a day of revolutionary equality in society. On that day all rest equally, regardless of wealth or power or need. Of course, the world is not ordered according to the well-being and equality of sabbath rest. But the keeping of sabbath, in heaven and on earth, is a foretaste and anticipation of how the creation will be when God's way is fully established. . . . As it is kept by the faithful week by week, sabbath is a disciplined reminder of how creation is intended.[33]

The christological focus of the doctrine of creation in the New Testament can also serve as a reminder that creation is centred on Jesus Christ, the incarnate Logos, and not on the human species. Although creation may seem a minor theme in the New Testament this is a misleading impression. Significant sections of the New Testament develop the Old Testament trajectory of creation traditions and demonstrate a deep continuity with the faith of Israel.[34] Jesus exercises the creative activity of God in his ministry, in the healing of the sick, the stilling of the storm and the raising of the dead. He is further identified as God's creative agent and the bringer of the new eschatological creation. He is described variously as wisdom, word, Adam, alpha and omega.

The designation of Jesus in this way not only leads to the development of the doctrines of Trinity, person and work of Christ, but also provides a christological intensification of the doctrine of creation. The Christ who fills the universe is the one who will call forth the praise of all God's creatures. The (deutero) Pauline epistles Ephesians and Colossians, with their cosmic strains, relate all creation across time and space to the risen and ascended Christ. Creation is here understood christocentrically rather than humanocentrically, even if human beings retain a central place by virtue of God's grace. At its best this should be seen not as a restricting of the activity of God in creation, but as the cosmic extension of the significance of the person and work of Christ. This point is made graphically in some words of Alan Lewis. We should remember, he writes,

> that grammatical colon at the end of the creed's first article, and ask whether everything we say of Christ and the Spirit has not to do with the making, and thus with the healing, remaking and final fulfilling, of heaven and earth. Is this not what the biblical drama is ultimately about? If the tragedy in this drama is that what God has made is broken, flawed, diseased, incomplete, under threat of death, is not the comedy, passing from

misery to felicity, that God has not abandoned the cosmos which he has made, but has acted and is acting through Christ and the Spirit to remake it, restore it to wholeness, so that at last, only at the end, will he have accomplished this and its original goal? ... Heaven and earth will not have finally been created until they have been remade, and everything that threatens, negates and destroys them has been forever removed.[35]

Creation and Redemption

One of the most compelling features of George MacLeod's Iona prayers is their juxtaposition of creation and redemption. The delight in the beauty of all created things is tempered yet intensified by a conviction of their imperfection. The presence of God in nature is accompanied by a sense of its need of redemption. 'Gladly we live in this garden of Your creating. But creation is not enough. Always in the beauty, the foreshadowing of decay.'[36] One finds a similar correlation of creation and redemption in Hopkins' poetry. It is no coincidence that Hopkins had immersed himself in the writings of the Greek Fathers. The creation is celebrated but everywhere it is seen to suffer corruption. It cries out therefore for the redemption which comes through the incarnation.

> The world is charged with the grandeur of God.
> It will flame out, like shining from shook foil;
> It gathers to a greatness, like the ooze of oil
> Crushed. Why do men then now not reck his rod?[37]

The God of grandeur is the God of Christ. The flames that shine from shook foil are the tongues of flame. They prefigure the poem's conclusion. The pentecostal fire is the Holy Spirit's communication of the risen Christ to the world. The oil is a symbol of abundance and of grace poured out.[38]

The task of relating creation and redemption is one that has always beset Christian theology. The challenge for a doctrine of creation is to speak of the goodness of the world, and the secular manifestation of God's grace yet without neglecting the particular events of revelation and reconciliation. The challenge for a doctrine of redemption is to avoid a narrow constriction of God's providential activity to the history of Israel and the Church, and the consigning of creation to a mere stage within which the redemption of an elect group is executed.

These difficulties are already present in the Old Testament with its different theological trajectories of creation and salvation.[39] The narrative and prophetic traditions assume that God is revealed in a series of historical events. These are characterized by such theological motifs as exodus, law and covenant. On the other hand, the wisdom literature of Job, Proverbs, Ecclesiastes, the Song of Songs and some of the Psalms assumes that God is apprehended in everyday life, in the general rather than the particular, in personal insight rather than national experience. Thus, the ancient sage can know of God and wisdom irrespective of the tradition of enquiry to which he or she belongs. The presence of both these trajectories in the canon demands theological attention. In any case, we can already discern attempts at integration in the canon itself.

That God's power and gracious activity extend over the whole created order is one reason for being open to wisdom in traditions and places other than one's own. It is also a reason for believing that God's concern is not limited to those within one stream of human history. At the same time, the wisdom literature also acknowledges its own limitations. There are elements of ambiguity and uncertainty that characterize human existence. For Qoheleth, a human being cannot discern what God means by it all. For Job, God can neither be resisted nor fully understood. God's final appearance is one which reveals the smallness of Job's own understanding. 'I had heard of you by the hearing of the ear, but now my eye sees you; therefore I despise myself, and repent in dust and ashes' (Job 42.5–6).

This limitation of knowledge and the dark side of creation signal the need for revelation. For the Psalmists, like George MacLeod, creation is not enough. Even Psalm 104 with its bright testimony to the harmony of nature speaks of the waters that have to be restrained, the darkness of the night, the death that awaits all creatures when the breath of God is withdrawn, and the travesty of the wicked who go unpunished. Psalm 19 directs one's attention not only to the starry skies above but to the perfect law of God which revives the soul. Job 28 asks where wisdom is to be found and responds that it resides only in the fear of the Lord. The order of creation is most fully manifested only in the life of God's redeemed people, a life of justice and social order regulated by the law. The equation between wisdom and law did not wait until the intertestamental period. It is already found in the Old Testament in Deuteronomy 4.5–6. 'See, just as the Lord my God has charged me, I now teach you statutes and ordinances for you to observe in the land that you are about to enter and occupy. You must observe them diligently, for this will show your wisdom and discernment to the peoples, who, when they hear all these statutes will say, "Surely this great nation is a wise and discerning people!" '[40]

In the New Testament this setting of the relationship between universal wisdom and particular historical revelation is achieved by the identification of Jesus Christ with God's wisdom and Logos. For Colossians, echoing Proverbs 8, the person of Jesus is identified with the wisdom through whom and for whom all things were made (Col. 1.15ff.). Christ is the one in whom are hidden all the treasures of wisdom and knowledge (Col. 2.3). The theology of ascension that one finds in Ephesians witnesses to Christ's indwelling of all things (Eph. 4.10). It is passages such as these that provide a way beyond what might be considered a christological constriction of God's wisdom and truth. It is true that if the creator is the Father, Son and Holy Spirit, then everything that the Father does in creation must be understood by reference to the work of the Son and the Spirit. But the converse also holds. Everything that the Son and the Spirit do must also be understood by reference to the creation of the world. Thus J. Wichelhaus, quoted approvingly by Karl Barth, once wrote, 'The glorification of God's name in Jesus Christ is accordingly the final goal of creation, so that everything is ordered for this purpose, and everything, be it light or darkness, good or evil, must serve this purpose.'[41]

When Barth spoke of creation as the external basis of the

covenant, and the covenant as the internal basis of creation, this
did not represent a narrowing of creation theology so much as
a universalizing of the significance of the person and work of
Christ. 'The doctrine of creation ... forbids us to think meanly
of Jesus Christ, his kingdom and his Church, as if the work of
our salvation and redemption were a kind of afterthought
which we might ignore in view of creation as God's first and
principal work.'[42] There are two implications of this worth com-
menting on. One is that the doctrine of creation is a specifically
Christian article of faith. It is not a vestibule of natural
theology nor a forecourt of monotheistic religion inhabited by
different faiths. 'To be a creature', Barth writes, 'means to be determined to this end, to be affirmed, elected and accepted by
God. To be a creature means to exist after the manner of Israel;
after the manner which God in His own Son has not deemed it
unworthy to adopt as His own. To be a creature means to be
prepared for the place where His honour dwells.'[43] A second implication of this linkage of creation and covenant is that even if
a free-standing natural theology unaffected by the presuppositions of positive religion is impossible, nonetheless a theology
of nature is imperative. The covenant embraces not merely a
few who are rescued from a perishing creation. It has as its goal
the entire created order, all of nature, animate and inanimate.

Dietrich Bonhoeffer perceived that in this sense Christianity is
a secular religion. It is a religion which is concerned with this
world in all its diversity, and not merely the Church as a
limited province of created reality. The grace of God in Christ
has the world as its goal and object. The kingdom of God,
rather than the saving of one's own soul, is the dominant
concern of the Old Testament. It is concerned not with a
distant world beyond but with this world as it has been
created, preserved and made subject in every aspect of its existence to God's law. The world to come, for which we hope,
exists for the sake of this world. In this sense, creation and incarnation, crucifixion and resurrection are intimately connected.[44]

—

CHAPTER TWO

Creation and Cosmology

Creation out of Nothing

The doctrine of creation out of nothing is not explicitly taught in Scripture. The opening chapter of the Bible seems to presuppose a formless waste out of which the heavens and the earth are created. Other passages in the Bible hint at the notion of God creating out of nothing, (e.g. Rom. 4.17; Heb. 11.3) as does the verse often cited from the Apocrypha. 'I beg you, my child, to look at the heaven and the earth and see everything that is in them, and recognize that God did not make them out of things that existed' (2 Macc. 7.28). It is not clear, however, that even here we have the doctrine of creation out of nothing as this has traditionally been understood. In speaking about nothing, these passages may not be referring literally to nothing. In the ancient world that which is not may simply mean that which has no character.[1] While this is clearly an expression of the sovereignty and power of God which was later elaborated in the idea of creation out of nothing, it is not certain that this was in the mind of the writer of 2 Maccabees. It is better to assume that we do not find creation out of nothing as an explicitly taught doctrine until the time when the Church contested the ancient Greek assumption about the eternity of matter.

It is difficult from a vantage point almost two millennia later to understand the counter-intuitive character of the doctrine of creation out of nothing. Most of us were so well instructed in the notion that God made everything not from something but from nothing, that we find the notion of the eternity of matter both unimaginable and incredible. We thus lose sight of the novelty of the idea of *creatio ex nihilo* in the second century. The prevailing assumption was that matter was eternal, and that God, in creating the world, had imposed a shape upon that primordial substance. This is neatly explained by Jostein Gaarder in his best-selling novel on the history of philosophy, *Sophie's World*. 'Parmenides (*c.*540–480 BCE) taught that everything that exists had always existed. This idea was not alien to the Greeks. They took it more or less for granted that everything that existed in the world was everlasting. Nothing can come out of nothing, thought Parmenides. And nothing that exists can become nothing.'[2]

The classical statement of this view is found in Plato's *Timaeus*, a highly significant philosophical text for the theologians of the early Church. 'God desires that all things should be good and nothing bad, so far as this was attainable. And so finding the whole visible sphere not at rest, but moving in an irregular and disorderly fashion, out of disorder he brought order, considering that this was in every way better than the other.'[3] Justin Martyr writing around the middle of the second century was content to regard Plato as merely reproducing an idea found in Genesis, creation out of pre-existent matter. In his *First Apology*, Justin even claimed that Plato must have had access to the teaching of Moses in describing the fashioning of the world in the *Timaeus*. Thus he thought he could detect the Bible in Plato, even if he was inadvertently doing the reverse.[4]

Why was the eternity of matter such a widely shared presupposition of the ancient world? Richard Sorabji has conveniently summarized a series of arguments that can be detected in Parmenides, Aristotle and others.[5] These are mostly closely related arguments against the world having a beginning. One consideration is the 'why not sooner?' argument. A delay in an effect coming about is explained by reference to an earlier causal sequence. Thus Socrates could not have been born before his parents met. But there is nothing prior to the entire universe which can explain why it came to be when it did and not earlier. This argument is reinforced by considerations about the divine will. God's will is sufficient for the universe to come into being. Thus if God had eternally willed the universe it must have existed through all eternity, since an effect cannot be delayed when all its sufficient conditions obtain.

Further arguments relate to the changelessness and activity of

God. For motion to have had a beginning there must be a trigger mechanism, some prior motion, which brings this about. Yet if God is beyond change, God cannot provide at a particular point in time the necessary impetus for the beginning of the universe. This would result in God changing from potential to actuality with respect to that movement. Alongside this there is a presumption against the idleness of God. God cannot be inactive or indolent. God is eternally provident, according to Plato in ruling the cosmos. Indeed there is in Philo and the Christian tradition a related view that God presides over a timeless heavenly world and is therefore never doing nothing.

Perhaps the most powerful antidote to serious consideration of creation out of nothing was simply the view that 'nothing comes from nothing'. Sorabji claims that this principle was accepted by almost everyone outwith the Judaeo-Christian tradition. Parmenides argued that one cannot speak or think intelligibly of nothing, and Aristotle claimed that nothing can come to be from what is not. When a bronze statue is created, the bronze matter must exist before the change of form imposed by the sculptor.[6] (Aristotle did however concede that a form could come from nothing, and John Philopponus was later to ask why not matter also. In arguing with the neo-Platonists he claimed that there was no logical reason why creation could not come out of nothing.)

In this intellectual milieu, what is perhaps most surprising is that the doctrine of creation out of nothing came so quickly and with so little controversy to be the accepted teaching of the Church. Gerhard May in his important study of its emergence identifies Theophilus of Antioch and Irenaeus as the two key founders of the doctrine in the face of Gnostic speculation and Greek philosophy. May argues that in view of the definite and almost formal expression of the idea of creation out of nothing, Theophilus is articulating a view that has already become settled at Antioch. However, Theophilus goes on from this to present several arguments in favour of the doctrine.[7] If matter exists eternally alongside God, then God cannot be regarded as the creator of everything. If, like God, matter is unoriginate then to that extent it must be regarded as godlike. The sovereignty and power of God reside in God's having created the world out of nothing. Creation out of pre-existent matter would not reflect the greatness of God. (This is reminiscent of Thomas Aquinas's later argument that a universe with a beginning is a more fitting tribute to the goodness and power of its Maker. Aquinas believed, following Aristotle, that an eternal creation was possible but that Scripture – its revealed truth was not available to the ancient philosophers – declared otherwise. 'God's might and goodness are especially made manifest in that things others than Himself were not always.'[8]) On the basis of these considerations about divine power, Theophilus affirms his conviction that the matter of Genesis 1.2, out of which God shaped the cosmos, was itself brought into being by God from out of nothing. Creation is thus a two-stage process in which formless matter is first created and then receives the form imposed upon it by God.

Irenaeus further develops the distinction between the unoriginate God and the originate world. This excludes any notion of the creation emanating from God. If we see the world or any intermediate agent as proceeding from God then we introduce composition and change into the divine being. In describing the will of God as the sole ground of creation Irenaeus defends the freedom and omnipotence of the biblical God. Creation out of nothing is put forward as the only acceptable Christian alternative to pagan ideas of the eternity of matter and the emanation of the world from the being of God. Thus May concludes his discussion with the following summation.

> The contribution made by Irenaeus and Theophilus must not be underestimated: they developed the doctrine of *creatio ex nihilo* with such convincing stringency that from the end of the second century it becomes with astonishing speed the self-evident premise of Christian talk of the creation. We have to see in Theophilus and Irenaeus the specific founders of the church doctrine of *creatio ex nihilo*.[9]

It might further be noted that to speak of creation out of nothing is simply to say that creation is not out of something. The doctrine does not imply that 'nothing' has a kind of shadowy status which conditions a world that emerges from it. Attempts to explain the threat of evil in the cosmos by reference to the nihil of creation imply a return to quasi-pagan notions. Moltmann's treatment of creation out of nothing, though imaginative and moving, is ultimately unconvincing. In his Gifford Lectures he reinterprets creation out of nothing through Isaac Luria's cabalistic doctrine of *zimsum*. Zimsum means concentration and contraction. It signifies God's withdrawal into the divine being, as it were, and the consequent creation of a nothingness in which creation has its finite being. The idea of making room or letting-be is central to this notion. God, in withdrawing into the divine self by an act of self-retraction, creates the space within which other beings can have their freedom.

The status of this nothing assumes for Moltmann a negative character. 'The nihil in which God creates his creation is God-forsakenness, hell, absolute death; and it is against the threat of this that he maintains his creation in life.'[10] The attraction of this idea is that it immediately links creation and redemption, and this is powerfully explored by Moltmann. The creation from the outset is menaced by a nothingness which God must overcome to be 'all in all'. Yet the difficulty here is that evil seems to be explained as a necessary feature of the creation of anything that is not God. Moltmann comes close to the Hegelian position of equating evil and finitude. His use of *zimsum* is an attempt to explain the incursion of evil in the world by seeing this as a necessary condition of the world's finitude, as an inevitable consequence of its creaturely status. This makes problematic any notion of the goodness of creation. The Fall now becomes an integral feature of the very act of creation. The opening narratives of the Bible, however, are an attempt to distinguish between the creaturely status of the world and the universal presence of evil. Evil in the form of nothingness is not a metaphysically necessary implication of creation. By adding rather awkwardly the comment '[a]dmittedly the *nihil* only acquires this menacing character through the self-isolation of created beings to which we give the name of sin and godlessness', Moltmann reveals the weakness of this position.

The language of a divine self-retraction which creates a realm of nothingness is highly elusive and seems to presuppose a prior space which God can evacuate for the sake of creating a world. Any such notion of a pre-existent entity is precisely what is excluded by the doctrine of creation out of nothing. The nothing denotes not something, rather than a shadowy ontological realm which somehow menaces creation. We should resist the temptation of overloading nothing with metaphysical content, and take it merely to denote 'not something'. What it means to speak of creation out of nothing is most neatly summarized by Tertullian. Since the world does not proceed from the being of God and since the world has not existed eternally, God must have created it not out of something but out of nothing. The *nihil* refers primarily to the possibilities it excludes.[11]

Similar considerations can be found in Jewish and Islamic writers, although there has perhaps not been as strong a drive towards doctrinal orthodoxy in these faiths. The rabbinical commentators of the early centuries BCE were conscious that Genesis 1 seemed to imply the presence of something before the creation of the heavens and the earth. Moreover, Proverbs 8.22 – The Lord created me at the beginning of his work – was interpreted as referring to the pre-existence of the Torah. Jewish exegesis was able to argue that prior to the creation there were entities other than God, but that ultimately these had been created out of nothing.[12] In the Middle Ages, Maimonides opposed Aristotle's view of the eternity of matter by proposing an account of creation out of nothing. His argument, which appeals to the sovereignty of God, bears strong similarities to arguments found within the Christian tradition.[13]

One can also detect parallels between Christianity and Islam in the development of the doctrine of creation out of nothing, despite similar scriptural latitude on this theme. Islamic theologians were generally of the view that God had called the universe into being out of nothing. This seemed to follow from the assertion in the Qur'an (40.57/59) that God had made the heavens and earth from nothing, unlike human beings who had come from previously existing material. Yet the Qur'an (21.30/31) can also speak about the heavens and the earth coming from an undifferentiated mass of matter. Like the Hebrew Bible, we should probably not expect explicit doctrinal definition on this point in the Qur'an. 'The refinements of thought presupposed in an understanding of absolute non-existence were foreign to those who first heard Muhammad's preaching at Mecca and Medina.'[14] On the other hand, it is clear why Muslim theologians were favourably disposed towards creation out of nothing. The absolute being of God was unrivalled by any created thing, and everything owed its existence to the purpose and will of God. Al-Ghazali (1058–1111) argued against Avicenna that, under the influence of neo-Platonism, he had contradicted the tenets of Islam by *inter alia* teaching the eternity of creation. In a creed intended for the instruction of young Muslims he affirms creation out of nothing on traditional grounds.

> There is no existent apart from God, except what is originated by His act and proceeds from His justice; and that is the finest, most perfect, most complete and most just of manners . . . What is apart from God – human beings, jinn, angels, demons, the heaven and the earth, animals, plants and inanimate objects, substance and accident, what is perceived and what is sensed – all this is originated. By His power, God brought it into being after its non-existence, and made it something after it had been nothing, since from eternity He alone was existent and there was nothing along with Him . . . He did this not because of any lack of it or need for it.[15]

Although the three Abrahamic faiths could share a common interest in defending creation out of nothing, there were also strong trinitarian reasons within Christian theology for affirming the doctrine. In his history of dogma, Jaroslav Pelikan points out that while the conflict with paganism had led to the doctrine of creation out of nothing this was made even more crucial by the subsequent conflict with Arianism.[16] The heretical assertion of the creaturehood of the Son led to a sharper distinction between the eternal origin of the Son and the creation of everything that was not God. Already in Irenaeus we see a distinction between the begetting of the Son by the Father and all creaturely processes. There is no emanation from God. To hold to such a view is to make God composite and divisible. The will of God rather than the nature of God is the sole cause of creation, and the coming into being of the creation is to be distinguished from the eternal relations of origin within the Godhead. This was worked out primarily with reference to the Father–Son relation. From the perspective of the the doctrine of creation it was unfortunate that the New Testament identification of Wisdom, Word and Son led in subsequent theology to a neglect of the role of the Spirit. In the Old Testament we read frequently of the creative role of God's *ruach*. Its later restriction to a communication of the work of Christ often led theologians, particularly in the Latin West, to neglect the role of the Spirit in the creation, sustaining and redeeming of the natural world.[17] Nonetheless, in the Eastern Church there has been a greater recognition of the creator Spirit. In Basil of Caesarea's *De Spiritu Sancto*, the Holy Spirit is described as the one who brings to perfection all that is made by the Father through the Son. 'And in the creation bethink thee, first, I pray thee, of the original cause of all things that are made, the Father; of the creative cause, the Son; of the perfecting cause, the Spirit; so that the ministering spirits subsist by the will of the Father, are brought into being by the operation of the Son, and perfected by the presence of the Spirit.'[18]

Nicene orthodoxy thus intensified the issues surrounding the origin of the world, and led both to a differentiation and to a co-ordination of the relations within the Trinity and the creation of the universe. T. F. Torrance summarizes how this was worked out in his discussion of Nicene theology in *The Trinitarian Faith*. Three main points can be noted.

1. God was not always Creator. The Son is eternally begotten of the Father and is without beginning. The Son and the Spirit are generated by the nature of God, but the world by God's

will. If God was not always Creator, the creation of the universe as reality 'external to God' was something new in the eternal life of God. Together creation and incarnation conflicted sharply with Greek philosophical categories of the necessity, immobility and impassivity of God.

2. God does not will to exist for God alone. Creation, like redemption, must be seen as a sheer act of God's inexplicable grace exhibited in the incarnate Son. God was free to create the universe, but God was also free not to create it. Yet it has an ultimate rational ground in the beneficent nature and love of God. The creation is a temporal analogue of the love within God.[19]

3. The contingence of creation. The universe is not self-supporting or self-sustaining. Its character is not determined by the being of God. (God need not have created this world.) As contingent it is vulnerable to change, decay and the threat of non-being. Creation is restored from its fallenness, a consequence of contingence, by the incarnation of the word.

The doctrine of creation out of nothing enabled Christian theologians to distinguish the necessary God from the contingent creation. There could be no confusion of the different ontological statuses of these. In this respect, the doctrine can be construed as biblical even if not explicitly taught in Scripture. Creation is the result of the divine will. It is a free but unnecessary act for God. It also has the function of avoiding any ultimate dualism in Christian theology. God and the world are not antithetical forces. The one is made to serve the other. Thus Tillich remarked, 'This negative meaning of *creatio ex nihilo* is clear and decisive for every Christian experience and assertion. It is the mark of distinction between paganism, even in its most refined form and Christianity, even in its most primitive form.'[20]

The doctrine of creation out of nothing was accepted, it seems, almost immediately and unanimously. It held sway for centuries. And yet we encounter today a range of criticisms of the doctrine. What are we to make of these? I shall argue finally that these are not cogent but that they do point to some puzzling aspects of the doctrine, and thus are a measure of its limitations.

According to process theology, the traditional doctrine renders God's freedom in creating the world arbitrary. It suggests that God might not have chosen to create the world. This, however, makes divine creativity contingent rather than a necessary feature of God's existence. This is typically rejected by process thinkers. Where God is thought of as eternally personal and loving we must assume that there are from all eternity objects to which God can relate creatively. It thus makes no sense to think of God as having been without a world, or as not requiring a world in order to be God. To speak of the eternal love within the Trinity will not do. 'A kind of mutual admiration fellowship of the members of the Trinity seems unworthy of the proper object of worship.'[21]

If we cannot think coherently of God without the world, then the doctrine of creation out of nothing must be abandoned. The world is co-eternal, albeit dependent upon God. For process theology, God needs the world in that God must always be responsive. The world for its part cannot be understood except in relation to the indefatigable purposes of God. In this respect, the doctrine of *creatio ex nihilo* is rejected.[22] The doctrine of creation must be replaced by a doctrine of creating. God does not bring the universe into being from nothing, but God does seek to create within the universe values which correspond to the divine being. Process theology typically perceives this as the creation of order out of chaos. It is the creation of patterns of order which realize values such as consciousness, pleasure, freedom, and love. God is not an absolute controller but one who works with the raw materials that lie to hand in order to bring about enduring individuals from random low grade occasions.[23]

The problem with this is that it tends towards absolutizing the world. Creation is reduced to God's creative activity within the world. God is active but not in the sense of creating the raw materials of the universe. It has neither origin nor explanation, but is as brute a fact as the existence of God itself. The world – if not this one, then the series of worlds which preceded it and to which it belongs – must be regarded no longer as finite but as enjoying the same eternal duration as God. Yet, as Moltmann argues, this effectively denies the doctrine of creation by reducing it to the doctrines of preservation and providence.[24] It also modifies the manner in which God rules the universe, thus calling into question traditional notions of divine action and eschatology. With the loss of any notion of the beginning of creation, there is a consequent loss of any sense of an ending.

Yet difficulties persist with the notion of the freedom of God in the *ex nihilo* tradition. The implication that God might not have created the world, had God chosen not to do so, seems to render creation a capricious act. In doing so it fails to give account of the way in which God is irrevocably bound to the world. John Macquarrie registers this concern in arguing that too much stress was given to divine freedom in the traditional understandings of creation. The model of creating, he claims, needs to be balanced by a model of emanation. Given the divine nature there is a kind of internal necessity in the creation of the world. A similar desire to accommodate the theme of emanation can be detected in Moltmann who, though not a process thinker, may be thought of as a panentheist. The doctrine of emanation which sees the world as the overflow of the divine nature was too easily dismissed as Gnostic or Neoplatonic.

> It is more appropriate if we view the eternal divine life as a life of eternal, infinite love, which in the creative process issues in its overflowing rapture from its trinitarian perfection and completeness, and comes to itself in the eternal rest of the sabbath. It is the same love, but it operates in different ways in the divine life and in the divine creativity. This distinction in God makes it possible to preserve the distinction between God and the world in all the different forms which the communion between them takes.[25]

These attempts to understand creation as an act which expresses the divine nature are proper. The freedom and love of God ought not to be viewed apart from one another. To describe creation as an act of pure will without reference to the divine essence of love is to hint at a randomness and indeterminacy in the doctrine of God. This is rightly challenged by the Nicene observation that the creation of the world corresponds to, though is not demanded by, the nature of God. But notions such as overflowing and emanation effectively depersonalize the act of creation. Freedom, will and intention are all concepts that belong to the personal mode of discourse, and these are largely lost sight of in an emanationist model of creation. Pannenberg in his recent *Systematic Theology* criticizes Moltmann for this very same reason. He argues that creation as a free act of love must be articulated on trinitarian lines. The goodness of the Father towards creation reflects the love that the Father has from all eternity for the Son in the Spirit, and which is rendered back to the Father by the Son in the Spirit. Creation is thus consistent with the eternal love and being of God. It is not a random act of will but a free expression of the personal love within the triune being.[26] Eberhard Jüngel sets out a further reason for maintaining the distinction between the eternal relations of the Trinity and the temporal derivation of the world. The grace, the unmerited favour, that establishes a relation between God and the world is recognized by maintaining a distinction between the Son's coming eternally from the Father and the human creature's coming temporally from God.[27]

One unresolved difficulty in much of this discussion is whether the freedom of God in creation implies that God could have chosen not to have created the universe. This construction of divine freedom certainly seems arbitrary. It should probably not be placed upon the notion of creation out of nothing. Yet creation as a free act needs to be maintained if the personal, creative and gracious initiative of God is to be understood. If we cannot explicate divine freedom any further we might recall the difficulties philosophers and theologians have had explicating human freedom. If freedom in our own case is an opaque notion we should not be over-anxious if divine freedom is also.

There is more than a mere playing with words here. There is much at stake in the way in which we conceive of the relationship between God and the world. The *ex nihilo* tradition may have stressed too heavily the power and sovereign will of God, but there were strong religious reasons for protecting these in the first place. The transcendence and freedom of God were necessary conditions for divine interaction with the creation. In articulating the otherness of God the *ex nihilo* tradition also sought to make sense of biblical themes of covenant, incarnation, redemption and eschatological consummation. These are predicated upon the possibility of divine interaction with the creation. The idea of emanation, however, tends to substitute an organic model of creation for this more personal model. The concepts of divine freedom, intention and agency are difficult to sustain where the life of God is part of the process of the cosmos. By failing to distinguish adequately the nature of a necessary God from the nature of the contingent world, an interactive relationship between the two, characterized by patterns of freedom and intention, is difficult to accommodate.

The philosopher John Macmurray points repeatedly in his writings to the difference between material, organic and personal forms of activity. At the organic level activity takes the form of life adapting itself spontaneously to the purposes of life. At the personal level free activity takes place upon the basis of knowledge, appreciation and the desire for communion with other beings. Personal freedom is possible only where persons are distinct and not parts of a single organic process.[28] The shift in much recent theology towards models of emanation and immanence has lost sight of the way in which it is precisely the ontological distancing of God and the world that is necessary for their being related in a particular way. This leads to a depersonalizing of the God–world relationship which is inimical to many of the central themes of the Christian religion. In this respect, the transcendence and immanence of God are mutually dependent, rather than exclusive notions. The otherness of God is a necessary condition of the grace of God. The sheer gratuitousness of creation is a necessary condition of its contingency. The sovereignty of God is a necessary condition of the divine self-abasement in the incarnation. The drift towards exclusively immanentist patterns of thought in contemporary theology makes it hard to accommodate those aspects of God and God's activity for which Scripture and tradition have used personal language.[29]

The Cosmological Proof

The doctrine of creation out of nothing is a doctrine that has been commended not only for theological reasons. It has been argued that philosophically this doctrine gives the only sufficient answer to the ancient question 'Why is there something rather than nothing?' The cosmological argument takes different forms, but in essence its appeal to creation out of nothing is based on considerations of simplicity and explanatory power. Two main forms of the arguments can be found in Islamic and Christian thought.[30] The so-called Kalam cosmological argument (*Kalam* is the Arabic word for 'speech' which came to denote a particular school of philosophical theology in medieval Islam) argues from our knowledge of temporal, causal regress to the conclusion that God is the efficient cause of the universe. It was developed by several Muslim thinkers, who may have borrowed it from John Philopponus. From the principle that every event must have a prior cause, it is argued that the world itself must have a prior cause, namely God. Only the personal will of God is an adequate causal explanation for the world taking the form it did. The difficulty with this argument as a proof is that it is hard logically to exclude an ever-lasting temporal series of causes stretching endlessly backwards. It is also difficult conclusively to refute the hypothesis that the world may have had no efficient cause, i.e. it sprang into being uncaused.

Another version of the cosmological argument, also found in Muslim thinkers of the Middle Ages, appeals to the notion of God as the only adequate explanation of the world. This is not an argument based on the temporal regression of causes. It is based on the wider notion of rational explanation. It claims that only a necessary God can account for a contingent universe whether or not this universe has a beginning in time. The most celebrated version of this argument is found in the

German rationalist philosopher, Leibniz (1646–1716). Leibniz appeals to a principle which asserts that nothing happens without a sufficient reason for it being so and not otherwise. This is known as the principle of sufficient reason. In our everyday life we employ this principle and it is frequently verified by our findings. Historians, detectives and doctors in their professional activities search for sufficient explanations of the phenomena which confront them. If none can be found, this is assumed to be a result of human ignorance rather than the objective absence of explanatory reasons. According to Leibniz, the world as a whole requires an explanation because it might have been different and indeed might not have existed at all. The only complete and final explanation available is God, who must be eternal and necessary in being, otherwise God too will require an explanation. Thus the final resting-place for an explanation of everything, an answer to the question of why there is something and not nothing, must be God. This argument looks impressive but is it conclusive? Can it refute the tough-minded opponent, like David Hume, who simply denies that the universe itself must have a sufficient explanation.

To posit a divine creation *ex nihilo* is to offer an account of the universe which can explain what on any other hypothesis remains unexplained. The God hypothesis is to be preferred because it is simpler and has greater explanatory power than the rival view that the universe or some form of primordial matter is merely a brute fact. The most accessible defence of this argument can be found in the recent writings of Richard Swinburne. Swinburne does not argue that the cosmological argument is deductively valid. Instead, he claims that it is valid inductively to the extent that it contributes to the likelihood of God's existence. Traditional theism – a term which includes Judaism, Christianity and Islam – has massive explanatory power in being able to account for the existence, order and character of the entire cosmos. It possesses simplicity in that it postulates a single cause, namely God, who has infinite knowledge, power and freedom. God's infinite attributes may be considered simple to the extent that there are zero limits to the possession of these.

So there is our universe. It is characterized by vast, all-pervasive temporal order, the conformity of nature to formula, recorded in the scientific laws formulated by humans. It started off in such a way (or through eternity has been characterized by such features) as to lead to the evolution of animals and humans. These phenomena are clearly things 'too big' for science to explain. They are where science stops. They constitute the framework of science itself. I have argued that it is not a rational conclusion to suppose that explanation stops where science does, and so we should look for a personal explanation of the existence, conformity to law, and evolutionary potential of the universe. Theism provides just such an explanation.[31]

There is, I think, something in this argument. But the problem is that it is difficult to assess precisely how much. It claims with some force that the doctrine of creation out of nothing can explain what on alternative accounts must remain an inexplicable mystery. To this extent it has cogency. It is less easy, however, to determine what degree of probability it should be accorded. There are by the very nature of the case no background considerations or precedents to assess levels of probability. A further problem attaches to the notion of simplicity. Is a being with unlimited powers a simple explanation? On other criteria, this might be considered the least simple hypothesis available since it postulates an entity so radically different from all other known entities. Finally, this argument for the explanatory power of theism stumbles against the problem of evil. Would a universe constructed by a being of moral goodness and power contain such significant levels of natural and moral evil?

I suspect that Swinburne's argument can confirm the views of those for whom the very existence of the universe is a sheer mystery. It indicates that the only complete explanation of the world lies beyond it in God. It was said of Wittgenstein that he sometimes had a certain experience which could best be described by saying that 'when I have it, I wonder at the existence of the world. I am then inclined to use such phrases as "How extraordinary that anything should exist!" or "How extraordinary that the world should exist!" '.[32] For this intuition of the strangeness of being, the cosmological argument might have some force. For those who have some sense of Hopkins' inscape, and who marvel at the 'thisness', the distinctiveness and pattern of the physical world, the argument may set out a kind of religious intuition. Yet there are others who perceive no need to explain the world by reference to anything beyond it. For them the argument has little force. Consider these remarks of Richard Dawkins.

> It is a virtue of clear writing that you can see what is wrong with a book as well as what is right. Richard Swinburne is clear. You can see where he is coming from. You can also see where he is going to, and there is something almost endearing in the way he lovingly stakes out his own banana skin and rings it about with converging arrows boldly labelled, 'Step here'. It is surprising that a writer as clear as Swinburne has risen to the top of his profession. Theology is a field in which obscurantism is the normal path to success. . . . A God capable of continuously monitoring and controlling the individual status of every particle in the universe is not going to be simple. His existence therefore is going to need a modicum of explaining in its own right.[33]

This invective is hardly fair to Swinburne. Yet it does point to the limitation of this type of apologetic argument. To those who already hold to a belief in creation, it will make good sense. The existence of God can explain what otherwise is an astonishing fact. Yet for others, who perceive no ultimate significance or purpose within the universe, the argument will not convince. It will merely generate fresh problems and a different kind of astonishment that God should have no explanation.

The Big Bang Theory

In this context, it is worth considering the doctrine of creation out of nothing in the light of recent cosmology. Debates earlier this century between the competing models of the big-bang and the steady-state theories of the universe have now

turned in favour of the former. The hypothesis that the
universe began in a great fireball from a single point of
infinite density is widely accepted. It has been confirmed by.
three fundamental observations.[34] (a) The speed at which the
galaxies are moving away from us and the universe expanding
is explained by an original big bang which must be dated to
about 15 billion years ago. (b) Background radiation signals
which come from everywhere across the universe can be explained as coming from an initial fireball after 15 billion years
of 'wandering around the universe had cooled it down'.
(c) The big bang can also explain the measure of ingredients
that are found throughout the universe. Thus an explosion of
unimaginable heat which cools down within a few minutes
created the nuclear conditions under which 75 per cent of
atoms are hydrogen, 25 per cent helium, with a little deuterium
and lithium, etc.

Big-bang cosmology is one of the great intellectual achieve-
ments of our time. It provides a magnificent explanation of the
origins of our universe, its current condition, and its future
shape. In particular, its reflections upon the first milliseconds
of the universe's history describe in breathtaking manner the
processes which brought about galaxies, planets and different
life-forms here in earth. Borrowed from Ian Barbour,[35] the following table of the history of the cosmos provides a useful
overview of what is proposed by the big-bang theory.

Time	Temperature ($°C$)	Transition
15 billion years		(today)
10 billion years		Planets formed
1 billion years		Galaxies formed (heavy elements)
500,000 years	2000	Atoms formed (light elements)
3 minutes	10^9	Nuclei formed (hydrogen, helium)
10^{-4} seconds	10^{12}	Protons and neutrons formed from quarks
10^{-10} seconds	10^{15}	Weak and electromagnetic forces separate
10^{-35} seconds	10^{28}	Strong nuclear force separates
10^{-43} seconds	10^{32}	Gravitational force separates
(0	Infinite	Singularity?)

What is the theological status of this widely accepted theory? The most discussed treatment of the question is in Stephen Hawking's *A Brief History of Time*. Published in 1988 it had sold 5.5 million copies world-wide by 1993. It is hard to ascertain the secret of its success. It is a difficult read and much of the science is beyond the grasp of the non-specialist. Bernard Levin once confessed that he had never got beyond the first thirty pages, and reckoned that *A Brief History of Time* must be like the Bible. Most homes own a copy but it rests unread forever on the shelf. Perhaps the fascination with this book has something to do with the life-story of its author. Angela Tilby described her encounter with him in the following way.

> Stephen Hawking has become a wisdom figure of our age. His lopsided, smiling face and twisted form have replaced the face of Einstein as an icon of mental power and knowledge. He now speaks with the help of a computer-generated voice, in a robotic American accent. He is thus extraordinarily detached from time and relationship ... He survives, better than most people would, because he is intellectually gifted enough to be able to live in his mind. I asked him at one point whether he was ever angry or bitter about his illness. He reported that he did not really regard himself as disabled. 'When you are dealing with the workings of the universe a little mechanical difficulty in moving around and in speaking seems rather unimportant.' Heroism or denial? It is impossible to tell. Perhaps it is both.[36]

Hawking has attempted to show that the big bang theory does not demonstrably require the existence of God at a point before the coming to be of the initial singularity. His views have been widely circulated. It has been suggested that he has somehow made God redundant. It is doubtful whether Hawking himself thinks this, but it is a view pedalled in Carl Sagan's introduction to his book. There he suggests that Hawking has shown that a universe with no edge in space, and no beginning or end in time is one in which there is nothing for a Creator to do.

Hawking tells of how he attended a conference hosted by the

Vatican in 1981. The Pope had instructed scientists that it was improper to enquire into the explanation for the big bang since this was the moment of creation and therefore the work of God. At the same conference, Hawking put forward the idea that time and space formed a surface that was finite in size but without boundary or edge. The universe thus has no initial locus. It is self-contained and in no need of divine explanation. 'So long as the universe had a beginning, we could suppose it had a creator. But if the universe is really completely self-contained, having no boundary or edge, it would have neither beginning nor end: it would simply be. What place, then, for a creator?'[37]

Hawking's proposal (like Guth's theory of inflation) is an attempt to take the oddity and idiosyncrasy out of the big bang. His remarks may reflect a conviction that standard big-bang cosmology with its implicit notion of time o (the concept of singularity) makes the postulation of God's existence inevitable. He is reported once to have said 'If there is an edge, you would really have to invoke God.'[38] His argument for a curved space–time dimension is an attempt to remove any sense of a spatial or temporal boundary to the universe. Thus, he tries to block off any easy inference to God. Perhaps this is as well since there has always been a danger in appealing to God to fill the gaps in scientific understanding. On the other hand, it would be wrong to think either that God can have no explanatory role to play, or that scientific can replace theological explanation. The concept of creation is not a postulate which is advanced when science breaks down. It is not an attempt to make good any gap or deficiency within scientific theory. It is rather an explanation of a different order which accounts for the entirety of the contingent universe and the whole scientific enterprise. Creation has never been treated as a single dateable event which can be traced by a cosmologist. Hawking's comments in this much-quoted section of his work are polemical and hyperbolic. Yet even for him the role of God is far from redundant. This is evident from comments he has made elsewhere. 'What is it that breathes fire into the equations and makes a universe for them to govern? Although science may solve the problem of how the universe began, it cannot answer the question: why does the universe bother to exist? I don't know the answer to that.'[39]

The traditional account of the God–world relationship does not make God a part of the temporal processes of the world. It claims that the whole spatio-temporal universe is contingent, and that it is dependent upon the creating and sustaining action of God. Creation, in this respect, is not the hypothesis of a dateable event which can be confirmed or disconfirmed by scientific theory. This has been a standard and legitimate response to Hawking.[40] On the other hand, it is a response which makes the Christian account of creation compatible with either big-bang cosmology or the steady-state theory. The dependence of the universe on God – by virtue of the divine preservation and sustaining – could be affirmed of one that stretches back endlessly in time, as well as of a universe with a beginning. This point was well made by E. L. Mascall when he remarked that creation as a timeless act can be either the creation of a world whose 'temporal measure has a lower boundary or the creation of world whose temporal measure has not'[41]. But does the consensus in favour of the big-bang cosmology facilitate a greater consonance between theology and science today? What theological difference, if any, does the big bang make?

The theological account of creation suggests that the universe had a beginning and that it will have an end. History is linear and finite, rather than cyclical and eternal. Modern science likewise suggests that the universe had a beginning, and that it will have an end whether it be the big crunch or a slow heat death. To this extent at least there is some convergence between theology and modern science, although much of the gain at the front end of this story is now lost at the far end. 'An eschaton wherein the entire universe becomes totally dissipated into an energyless and matterless plenitude is hardly the salvation proclaimed by Scripture.'[42] We shall consider this eschatological problem in more detail in the final chapter. Nonetheless, the contingent universe with a beginning and end, and a unidirectional flow of time makes better sense of the biblical world view than the eternal cosmos of the steady-state theory. This is not to say, of course, that God's creative work is exhausted by an initial action in which the universe is brought into being. This is an essential part of creation but it is not the whole picture, as in deism. The work of God continues through the history of the universe bringing it to its appointed end. In this respect, the classical notions of *creatio ex nihilo* and *creatio continua* are complementary rather than competitive notions.

There is no relationship of necessary entailment between big-bang cosmology and the doctrine of creation out of nothing. In this respect, science and theology offer explanations at different levels. Yet the consonance between the two can be perceived. This is stated with commendable caution by Ernan McMullin. 'If the universe began in time through the act of the creator, from our vantage point it would look something like the big bang cosmologists are now talking about.'[43] It is of course possible to postulate the existence of many other universes somehow behind or before this one, but as far as we know this is the only one that has existed.

The world view with which we are presented remains that of a finite system from which the history of the cosmos proceeds. The question of its origin if not its first event does not go away.[44] The second law of thermodynamics demands that we think in terms of a beginning and an end of the universe as we now know it in terms of galaxies, stars, planets and conscious life. What Hawking is attempting may be of considerable scientific interest but it is of little theological consequence. His cosmology does not take us back to the eternal universe of Aristotle or the steady-state theory, and even if it did it would not make redundant the question of whether the cosmos has an explanation or is merely a brute fact.

This point is brought into sharp relief by John Lucas. He argues that even if, as Hawking claims, it makes little sense in terms of the big-bang theory to ask what happened prior say to an initial quantum fluctuation, one might still see this as an intelligible question in terms of some other framework of temporal reference, e.g. God's time.

[S]ome of the physical parameters we correlate with the time during most of the universe's history – entropy or the spatial volume of the universe – cannot be extrapolated back before the Big Bang, so that we cannot ask quasi-temporal questions of them. But that does not mean that we cannot ask temporal questions at all. For time is not defined solely by reference to physical parameters, in respect of which it is a concomitant of change, but is linked with other non-physical concepts too, notably mental ones. The theist can perfectly intelligibly ask what God was doing before the Big Bang, and even the atheist can hypothetically imagine a disembodied intelligence at the time of the Big Bang and wonder what his experience would have been like.[45]

(This response, of course, predicates temporality of God and is thus at odds with the traditional view of God's timelessness. Augustine, in his response to the question of what God was doing before the creation of the world, considered first the whimsical retort that God was preparing hell for those who pry into mysteries. His more serious response, however, was that the question makes no sense since time only exists as an aspect of created reality. God, by contrast, is timeless.[46] This response, though, has come under attack in recent theology and philosophy of religion on the ground that it makes it difficult to predicate of a timeless being notions such as intention, action, knowledge, suffering and love which are central to the biblical conception of God.[47])

A further feature of the cosmos beyond its mere existence for which the doctrine of creation offers an explanation is its order and fruitfulness. Defenders of the so-called anthropic principle remind us that a universe like ours which can produce conscious life on planets circling stars requires a very finely tuned structure. A theory of divine creation can explain this in a way which seems unexplained if the cosmos is treated as a brute fact. We shall examine this in the next chapter.

CHAPTER THREE

===

Creation and Evolution

The Challenge of Darwinism

Of all known forms of life, only about ten per cent are still living
today. All other forms – fantastic plants, ordinary plants, living
animals with unimaginably various wings, tails, teeth, brains –
are utterly and forever gone. That is a great many forms that
have been created. Multiplying ten times the number of living
forms today yields a profusion that is quite beyond what I
consider thinkable. Why so many forms? Why not just one
hydrogen atom? The creator goes off on one wild, specific
tangent after another, or millions simultaneously, with an exu-
berance that would seem to be unwarranted, and with an abandoned energy sprung from an unfathomable font. What is
going on here? ... The question from agnosticism is, Who
turned on the lights? The question from faith is, Whatever for?[1]

These remarks of Annie Dillard from her novel *Pilgrim at Tinker
Creek* illustrate both the wonder and perplexity we experience
in surveying the history of life on our planet. The variety and in-
tricacy of life forms call forth our wonder. Yet the seeming
waste and harshness of this process raise questions. A striking
feature of the current debate on religion and science is the difference in attitude sometimes found between physicists and biologists. Many physicists impressed by the order, mathematical
elegance, and fine-tuning of the universe have rehearsed highly
sophisticated versions of the design argument for the existence
of God. Despite their differences one finds in the writings of
Paul Davies, John Polkinghorne, Ian Barbour and Russell
Stannard a readiness to consider sympathetically the explanations of religion for some of the most fundamental features of
the cosmos. On the other hand, amongst many biologists –

most notably, Richard Dawkins – one encounters scepticism and even hostility towards the assertions of theology. This has much to do with the perspective of evolutionary theory, which sees so much random change, pointless waste and violent suffering in the emergence of life on earth. Annie Dillard's questions sum up the contrasting perspectives of the physicist and the biologist. The physicist seems haunted by the question 'who turned on the lights?' while the biologist remains perplexed, asking, 'whatever for?'

Doubtless this is something of an over-simplification but it does not disguise the important contribution being made to our cultural self-understanding by scientists who can communicate with the general public. This point is made forcibly by John Brockman in his recent collection of essays by leading scientists, *The Third Culture*.[2] Our situation, he argues, is one in which literary intellectuals, having failed to make any serious encounter with modern science, have lost contact with the wider public through their obsession with the jargon-ridden theories of postmodernism. By contrast the running is now being made by leading scientists who seek to communicate directly with a public audience. Thus physicists, biologists, computer scientists and psychologists now produce books that sell heavily and which exercise an influence over popular culture.

Theology cannot avoid a serious engagement with contemporary science. Many church members spend their professional lives working within the natural sciences and ask significant questions of their faith. Moreover, the need to demonstrate the ability of theology to accommodate the best insights of other disciplines is an apologetic task necessitated by its realist truth claims. For Protestantism, however, evolutionary theory has provided a major challenge which has generally not been met in the most effective way. It has often been remarked that it was Roman Catholicism which had the greater difficulty with Galileo's heliocentric hypothesis but Protestantism which had the greater difficulty with Darwin.[3]

In the last chapter of his *Origin of Species* (1859) Darwin argued that he could explain the emergence and gradual perfection of new species on the basis of the variability of organs and instincts, and the struggle for survival which leads to the preservation of the most advantageous of these variations. Darwin did not invent the concept of evolution, and he first encountered the idea of natural selection from the philosopher Malthus. Yet he was the first to provide scientific evidence to support evolution by natural selection. His hypothesis had several advantages over the established Christian view that separate species had come into being by a special providential act of creation. Darwin's account could better explain the fuzziness in differences between species and varieties within them; it could explain anomalies such as the upland goose with webbed feet which were not used for swimming; and it could account for imperfect adaptation as in the case of a bee dying after using its sting or the ichneumonidae feeding inside the bodies of caterpillars.[4]

Darwinism attempted to explain the emergence of living organisms from common ancestors through principles of variation and adaptation. Under environmental pressure, the random physiological differences within species can confer an advantage in the struggle for survival. Those individuals possessing the most advantageous variations are more successful at surviving and reproducing. The subsequent population thus inherits these variations, and over a long period of time significant changes can be detected in the structure of the species. Today neo-Darwinism has developed these ideas through its improved understanding of the mechanisms governing genetic mutation. This follows the work of James Watson and Francis Crick in 1953 on DNA replication. This provided insight into the operation of genes and the manner in which hereditary characteristics are transmitted. Genetic variations can be transmitted through reproduction, thus determining the subsequent gene pool of a species. Neo-Darwinism now attempts to explain evolution at the macro-level by genetic mutation at the micro-level, in conjunction with the process of natural selection. While there are significant disagreements within biology as to whether these principles provide a complete explanation of the evolution of life, they are generally regarded as central elements of any comprehensive theory.

Neo-Darwinian theory seeks to explain the development of all living organisms on the basis of genetic mutation and natural selection. Living organisms evolve from common ancestors; multicellular organisms evolve from single-cell organisms, and it is further conjectured that these emerge from inanimate matter through the processes of organic chemistry. Much speculation is involved in explaining precisely how all this comes about, but as an overarching hypothesis it looks impressive. Provided nature has sufficient time most of these changes can be brought about. Modern cosmology now suggests that the earth is 4–5 billions of years old. Much of the incredulity which surrounds evolutionary theory can be dissipated by a better understanding of the timescales involved. Richard Dawkins gives the following example of the timescale in evolutionary history.

In a few hundreds, or at most thousands, of years we have gone from wolf to Pekinese, Bulldog, Chihuahua and Saint Bernard. ... Let's represent the total time it took to evolve all these breeds of dog from a wolf, by one ordinary walking pace. Then, on the same scale, how far would you have to walk, in order to get back to Lucy and her kind, the earliest human fossils that unequivocally walked upright? The answer is about 2 miles. And how far would you have to walk, in order to get back to the start of evolution on Earth? The answer is that you would have to slog it out all the way from London to Baghdad. Think of the total quantity of change involved in going from wolf to Chihuahua, and then multiply it up by the number of walking paces between London and Baghdad. This will give some intuitive idea of the amount of change that we can expect in real natural selection.[5]

The Creationist Controversy

To some the Darwinian challenge appeared to undermine several popular Christian beliefs: the authority of Scripture; the creation accounts of Genesis; the doctrine of the fall and Christ's redemption; the argument from design; the making of human beings in the image of God; the source and ground of moral values.[6] While many attempts were made to harmonize creation and evolution, or to modify Darwinism, we still see today a concerted effort to discredit the claims of evolutionary science. To a large extent, this is an American phenomenon. There are signs, however, that it will increasingly become an issue in Britain through the work of the Creation Science Movement, which superseded the Evolution Protest Movement in 1980, and also through the greater lobbying power of parents on school syllabuses. The CSM now disseminates information disconfirming evolution and provides speakers for colleges, universities, schools and church groups throughout the country. It exists to combat 'the hard nosed humanism' that has become entrenched in the British educational system.[7] Its regular publications offer a sustained and intense assault on many of the scientific orthodoxies of our day.

Creation science should not be lightly dismissed. It is politically significant, and many of its arguments against evolutionary theory are intellectually ingenious. Eileen Barker has commented that the literature produced by the leading creationists has a *prima facie* plausibility for the intelligent lay person. For those inhabiting 'socially protected world-views' who cannot readily marshall arguments against a wide-ranging attack on evolutionary theory, the creationist literature can be unsettling.[8]

Before looking at what creationists actually say, we should consider the historical roots of the movement. Conservative Protestant theology has not always been at war with theories of evolution. Even B. B. Warfield (1851–1921), the most formidable defender of Scripture's inerrancy, believed that creation and evolution were not mutually exclusive. Evolution, he argued, can at most be a 'method of divine providence'. So where did the intense opposition come from? Several socio-historical analyses have been offered and I shall simply cite a number of points from these.

Creationism has roots in Protestant convictions about the inerrancy of Scripture. The plenary theory of inspiration asserts the infallibility of Scripture on all matters on which it speaks: history, science, morals and religion. The Holy Spirit dictated the words to the writers in such a way as to exclude the possibility of any type of error. The insistence upon the most literal interpretation of the Bible possible is also a factor. This derives in part from premillennial thought with its predictions of the future based on readings of passages from Ezekiel, Daniel, Revelation and other difficult sections of Scripture. In deriving central beliefs from precise interpretations of prophetic and apocalyptic literature such groups are disposed towards a literal reading of the opening chapter of Genesis.[9]

Crucial to creationism is another Protestant conviction about the character of Scripture. The Bible is a book of propositional facts, it is a storehouse of information about the world, God and human beings. 'The Bible is filled with scientific statements of the same precision as might be found in twentieth-century journals. . . . One of the most common arguments against evolution of species is that Genesis One repeatedly says that plants and animals should produce "after their kind". This phrase is usually regarded as precluding one species ever producing another.'[10]

Many American citizens share what one sociologist has called 'an empirical folk epistemology' by virtue of which they tend to be incredulous of evolutionary hypotheses. Despite the support of scientific experts, evolution seems to contradict common sense. Many people lampoon it, as being a ludicrous and easily refuted aberration on the part of eccentric intellectuals. How could the amazing order and diversity of life have arisen from a primeval soup? How could elephants and insects possibly have evolved from a common source? Who has ever seen one species reproduce another very different species? In the face of evolutionary theory, the argument from design for God's existence seems more firmly rooted in common sense.[11]

What do creationists tend to say? There are major differences between creationists but the following are some typical claims of the more militant exponents.[12]

The stories in the Bible including Genesis 1—11 are to be understood as historical and scientific fact. There is little scope for parabolic or mythological exegesis. These narratives are not religious metaphors, they are literal fact and only as such can they speak to us of God. The universe is much younger than modern science suggests to us. The six days of creation plus the genealogies of the Bible enable us to date the universe to some-where around the 4004 BC suggested by Archbishop Ussher[13] at the beginning of the seventeenth century. Or, if you are willing to treat each of the six days as a thousand years in God's timescale, following Psalm 90.4, you might get a universe which is about 10,000 years old. Either way it is a much younger universe than the one that modern cosmology judges to be around 15 billion years old.

Creationists are also particularly committed to the historicity of the fall and flood stories in Genesis. The consequence of Adam's Fall and the Flood, which Noah and many animal species survived, is that the universe today is quite different from the one that was originally created. This appeal to the Fall and the Flood is used by creationists to explain some puzzling facts including the second law of thermodynamics, the extinction of species such as dinosaurs, and the prevalence of disease, suffering and death throughout life on earth. The second law is frequently invoked to explain the current disintegration of the cosmos. It is invoked as the effect of the Fall, thus enabling creationism to square the original goodness of creation with its current condition.[14]

By virtue of the above claims, creationism is at odds with current scientific orthodoxy. It contradicts the physics of the big-bang theory which dates the origin of the universe to an explosion many billions of years ago; it contradicts geological claims that rocks must be millions of years old, and that river and sea beds have taken millions of years to reach their present formation; it contradicts the tenets of palaeontology that many fossils must be dated as millions of years old; and it contradicts biological theories that species evolve and diverge through processes of natural selection and genetic mutation.

Creationism believes that theologically there is no alternative but to contest the claims of the aforementioned natural sciences. At stake is not only the credibility of the Bible, but the freedom, responsibility and morality that distinguish humans from the other animals. You cannot have both creation and evolution; these are mutually exclusive alternatives. Thus a theological crusade must be mounted against the secularism, humanism and infidelity of evolutionary theory. It is impossible to provide a comprehensive critique of creationism in this context, but the following considerations might help to show why, despite its ingenuity and resourcefulness, creationism is both scientifically untenable and theologically misguided.[15]

1. The big-bang theory is now widely accepted as an explanatory theory amongst physicists and cosmologists. It is supported by three principal considerations which were described in the last chapter: the speed at which the galaxies are moving away from us and the universe expanding; the background radiation signals which come from everywhere across the universe; the measure of ingredients that are found throughout the universe.

2. Since the work of Charles Lyell in 1830, geologists have maintained that the formation of rock strata and the earth's surface relief can be explained through the action of normal forces such as rivers, glaciers, waves and wind without recourse to a unique event such as a biblical flood. This can be done, however, only if the earth is millions of years old. It is worth noting that this hypothesis was put forward before the emergence of Darwin's theory of evolution and cannot therefore be construed as part of the evolutionary conspiracy. The technique of radiometric dating can now determine the age of a rock with reasonable reliability on the basis of the rate of decay of the original isotope into its daughter elements. This dates rocks from as young as 1 million years old to several billion years old. 'The overwhelming mass of interlocking data supporting the correctness of the results achieved by means of radiometric dating makes it clear why no professional geologist working on dating problems any longer has doubts about the validity of this technique.'[16]

3. Closely linked with the dating of rocks is the dating of the fossils embedded in them. Different combinations of fossils grouped together in strata of rocks reveal that living organisms were in a state of change with more advanced forms of

life appearing in the higher (and younger) strata. 'A unique combination of species apparently existed during each interval of geologic time, representative samples of which were fossilized and preserved in the rocks.'[17] We find in the creationist literature attempts to explain these phenomena by reference to a flood of biblical proportions which took place a few thousand years ago. Thus Henry Morris:

> Visualize, then, a great hydraulic cataclysm bursting upon the present world, with currents of waters pouring perpetually from the skies and erupting continuously from the earth's crust, all over the world, for weeks on end, until the entire globe was submerged, accompanied by outpourings of magma from the mantle, gigantic earth movements, landslides, tsunamis, and explosions. The uniformitarian will of course question how such a cataclysm could be caused, and this will be considered shortly, but for the moment simply take it as a model and visualize the expected results if it should happen today ... Sooner or later all land animals would perish. Many, but not all, marine animals would perish. Human beings would swim, run, climb, and attempt to escape the floods but, unless a few managed to ride out the cataclysm in unusually strong watertight seagoing vessels, they would eventually all drown or otherwise perish.[18]

These conjectures are bizarre and can be refuted by professional geologists and palaeontologists. Thus, for example, there is no evidence of any living vertebrate being found in the same rock strata as dinosaur fossils. This cannot be explained by reference to the way in which the Flood grouped and scattered perishing species. In any case to account for the extinction of so many species by appeal to the Flood is ironically to brand Noah a serious failure in carrying out the divine mission.[19]

4. The theory of evolution asserts that species have evolved through natural selection and genetic mutation. Is this part of the explanation of how human beings have come about?

The fossil evidence as interpreted by biology seems very strong. The progression from *homo australopithecus* to *homo africanus* to *homo habilis* to *homo erectus* to Neanderthal man to *homo sapiens* is impressively documented and illustrated in exhibitions such as the display in the Natural History Museum, London. Changes in fossils correspond to progression in time and differences in posture, teeth, forehead, brow, chin, and brain size. It is difficult to contest that we are as we are through a long process of evolution over a period of say 5 million years. Both natural selection and genetic mutation must have a role to play in explaining this process. Creationists tend to designate these creatures either as apes or as human beings, but the fact that they tend not to agree over *homo erectus* in the middle transitional period illustrates their difficulties.

In these aforementioned respects, physics, geology, palaeontology, and biology tend to confirm each other, and together provide a coherent view of the origin of the universe, and the history of our planet. Creationism is thus driven to contest the findings of mainstream science on a vast range of issues. It presents the consensus findings of modern science as a gigantic fallacy, unrivalled by any intellectual error in the history of culture. This is an impossible position to adopt, and in any case it is religiously unnecessary.

Genesis 1—11 contains not history and science as we understand these terms but a theological account of the origins of life and the status of the world and human beings as created. It does this by drawing upon concepts, images and stories from ancient Near-Eastern culture. It does not tell us *how* scientifically the world came to be as it is, but it does proclaim *that* God made the world and *why* God made it. It is entirely open for science to say that this came about through the big bang and the mechanisms of evolution. If religion is concerned with the *that* and the *why* of creation, there is in principle no incompatibility with the *how* of natural science.

The prospect of the legal enforcing of the teaching of creationism in American public schools has drawn some telling criticisms from a range of scientists and theologians.[20] It is the imposition of controversial religious dogma upon the public school system (dogma which none of the mainstream Christian denominations adheres to); it confuses the proper character of genuine scientific study; and it compromises the professionalism and academic freedom of teachers. Yet the increasing compartmentalization of our learning processes, the reactive nature of much of our religious life, and the disillusion with the result of modern science and technology threaten to bring these disputes nearer home in the UK. They will require to be met with informed and critical comment by teachers of both science and religion.

Dialogue with Evolutionary Theory

But what then of the more constructive engagement of theology and evolutionary theory? It should be made clear again that neo-Darwinism has not been confirmed as a complete explanatory hypothesis of how life has evolved on our planet. There remain problems and gaps within the theory which have yet to be resolved. These may require significant modifications of the theory.[21] For example, the gradualist assumptions of much evolutionary theory are hard to square with the story of uneven progress that seems to be told by the fossil records. In response to this problem, the most famous modification of neo-Darwinism is the theory of punctuated equilibria put forward by Niles Eldredge and Stephen Jay Gould.[22] Evolutionism, they claim, takes place not gradually but through episodes of rapid change which punctuate much longer periods of stability. A further problem with neo-Darwinism is whether it can adequately explain the progression towards greater complexity within the development of life-forms. Why should there be greater rather than less complexity under the random forces of genetic mutation and natural selection? Some theologians have ventured to argue that the rise of highly complex organisms from more primitive ones can only be explained by reference to a force other than genetic mutation or natural selection. This force is identified with divine action which is empirically undetectable.[23] While some may see this as too redolent of a God-of-the-gaps theory, it is significant that it does not eschew altogether the intersecting processes of random mutation and natural selection. These are still necessary, though insufficient, conditions for the development of life-forms. If so, it is incumbent upon the theologian to offer some rationale for the function of chance within the history of the universe. Whatever scruples one may have about neo-Darwinism as an exhaustive explanation, it is hard to deny that the mechanisms of natural selection and genetic mutation have played a crucial role in the evolution of life over millions of years. What responses then are available to theology?

The concept of chance has two applications in biological theory, both of which relate to the limits of predictability.[24] It can refer to small genetic mutations which are unrelated to the biological needs of the organism, or it can refer to the intersection of two unrelated causal schemes. In the first instance, chance refers to our ignorance of the conditions under which a mutated organism is selected and induced. This ignorance may not be the result merely of the lack of knowledge, since quantum considerations, which come into play at the submolecular level, entail that behaviour cannot be exactly predicted. In the second instance of chance, biological changes in organisms interact with the shifting physical environment. Thus changes in climate, supply of food, or fluctuations within other species can interact with changes in organism in the process known as natural selection. At this macro-level we now know that dynamic systems are also unpredictable. Even the smallest changes can significantly alter the behaviour of the entire system. The result of this is that the amount of information required increases dramatically in proportion to the level of predictability sought. It is humanly impossible to know exactly how dynamic systems will behave. The most notorious example is the weather system, which can be predicted only with a measure of accuracy. As the illustration of the fluttering of a butterfly's wings in the Amazon shows, even apparently insignificant events tilt the causal balance in ways that can be dramatic.

Perhaps the most dramatic example of chance in this second sense was the probable sudden disturbance of the ecosystem which led to the rapid extinction of dinosaurs about 65 million years ago. This may have been brought about by a meteorite's collision with the earth. As a consequence, human beings rather than reptiles dominate the planet today. When we speak of chance in either the micro- or the macro-levels we are not referring to events which lack explanation. We are dealing rather with events, the occurrence of which could not have been entirely specified on the basis of a knowledge of prior conditions. The concept of chance in this context draws attention to the measure of openness in the evolution of life. It points to spontaneity and novelty within the history of the universe. Its path conforms to the laws of science, yet it is not wholly determined by initial conditions and states.

Recent evolutionary critics of religion have argued that the role of chance effectively excludes any possibility of design or purpose in the history of life. Thus the French biologist Jacques Monod wrote in his famous *Chance and Necessity* (1970) that the history of life is unpredictable though not inexplicable for the same reason that the particular configuration of atoms in a pebble is unpredictable. We would like to think of ourselves as necessary, inevitable and ordained from all eternity. All our religion and most of our philosophy is an attempt to evade our contingency.[25] But modern biological explanation requires that we see the progress of life as essentially random and purposeless. What meaning there is arises only through heroic choice. 'The ancient covenant is in pieces; human beings know at last that they are alone in the universe's unfeeling immensity, out of which they have emerged only by chance. The kingdom above or the darkness below: it is for us to choose.'[26]

A similar attack on the doctrine of creation is found in the more acerbic criticism of Richard Dawkins, perhaps the most illustrious scientific critic of religion today.

If we want to postulate a deity capable of engineering all the organized complexity in the world, either instantaneously or by guiding evolution, that deity must already have been vastly complex in the first place. The creationist, whether a naive Bible-thumper or an educated bishop, simply postulates an already existing being of prodigious intelligence and complexity. If we are going to allow ourselves the luxury of postulating organized complexity without offering an explanation, we might as well make a job of it and simply postulate the existence of life as we know it! . . . The theory of evolution by cumulative natural selection is the only theory we know of that is in principle capable of explaining the existence of organized complexity.[27]

Dawkins' project is to show how chance can be tamed. Chance must be understood as a rational process which explains how things have come to be. This is done by breaking down the evolutionary process into a large number of infinitesimal changes through a period of time stretching over billions of years. Genetic mutation interacting with other causal processes in the environment can bring about astonishing levels of variety in the forms of life, provided that nature is given sufficient time and space in which to bring this about. Dawkins is a most formidable opponent of religion, yet it is far from clear that there is no room left for God on his account.

One response is to point to the metaphysical character of some of his utterances. Evolutionary theory can explain the emergence of life in its various manifestations, but to assert that neither matter nor the laws of science require any explanation is to make a claim of a very different sort. To argue from the explanatory power of evolutionary biology to the redundancy of metaphysical explanation is to commit a *non sequitur*. It remains at least a possibility that the facts of there being a universe at all and its government by the laws of natural science have an explanation. These are merely asserted as brute facts by Dawkins, his only supporting argument being that God must require an explanation as much as any universe does. His explanation of life presupposes the existence of inanimate matter out of which it could eventually emerge. It also presupposes the operation of the laws of biology, chemistry and physics upon this inanimate matter. These presuppositions must be made, but to assert that they are themselves without explanation is to have ventured

beyond the bounds of science.[28] Whether or not there is philosophical proof of God's existence, its possibility cannot be dis-
counted by natural science. In this respect science has nothing
to say about God. It cannot rule theological explanation out of
court.

Recent discussions of the so-called anthropic principle
suggest that the universe has a very fine tuning and delicate
balance which is necessary for life to evolve as we know it. In
the first milliseconds of its history it required a particular structure in order to produce stars, planets and conscious life on
earth. If the rate of expansion one second after the big bang
had been smaller or greater by one part in a million then either
the universe would have collapsed or it would have expanded
too rapidly for stars and planets to form. Without the fine
tuning of both the weaker and stronger nuclear forces, the chem-
icals necessary for life on earth as we know it could not have
arisen.[29] The big bang took place about 15 billion years ago.
The sun is some 5 billion years old, having evolved in the
Milky Way, a galaxy which began as a huge cloud of hydrogen
and helium, some 200,000 light years across. Planet Earth
seems to have formed some 4.5 billion years ago, along with
other planets, out of debris in space thrown up by an exploding
supernova. Thus the elements that make up our bodies have
come literally from the stars. All this does not prove that the
universe is designed, but it does at least raise its likelihood.
'The more I examine the universe and the details of its architec-
ture, the more evidence I find that the universe in some sense
must have known we were coming.'[30] A critic like Dawkins
who simply treats the universe and the laws of nature as brute
facts can have nothing to say about this. While it does not
provide compelling evidence of design it does at least point to
a significant feature of the universe which calls for explanation.[31]
One rejoinder might be to claim that this present universe is
simply one amongst many, and that its orderly structure is not
shared elsewhere throughout these multiple universes. Our perception of order everywhere is merely a function of our
location. This move might take away the oddity of our being
in such an orderly universe, but its postulation of numerous

alternative universes is extravagant and entirely without empirical support. For all we know, this is the only universe there has been.[32]

Divine Action

If we advert to God as the explanation of the laws of science, the existence of matter and the consequent emergence of life, what are we to make of God's intentions and involvement with the cosmos from our knowledge of the evolutionary process? The trend towards greater complexity and consciousness in the evolutionary process is compatible with some creative purpose. As new forms of life have emerged in the universe, so new categories of explanation become necessary. This hierarchy of levels of explanation is such that each new class of concepts emerges from and depends upon the class immediately below it. We thus proceed from physics through chemistry and biology to the social sciences. These latter are made possible by the emergence of consciousness and the creation of culture.[33] A simple action such as opening the door may require to be explained not only in terms of physics, chemistry and biology but also in terms of human purposes and social forms of life.

The effects of chance are such that they serve the drive towards greater complexity in the evolutionary process. In this respect, chance and law are complementary rather than competing forces in nature. This is claimed by David Bartholomew in his widely cited study *God of Chance*.[34] He argues that random events at one level may lead to statistical regularity at a higher level of aggregation. Redundancy and thresholds will limit the effects of random events on integrated systems and maintain order. Yet an element of randomness can produce change and movement. Chance is thus a condition of a fruitful universe in which new forms of life can emerge. Thus understood it is part of God's design and oversight rather than in conflict with it.

One possible response is to maintain theological determinism by insisting that what appear to be the effects of chance are explained by the hidden will of God.[35] Chance is only the way we perceive it from a limited perspective. In a complete explanation chance would be replaced by reference to the divine will or to some unperceived secondary causes which mediate that will. Nothing happens therefore that is not already built into the blueprint for the creation from the beginning. There is no scope for deviation from a predetermined course of events even through billions of years of evolution. This response could accommodate chance at the macro-level since a knowledge of the initial conditions governing systems which is in practice unavailable to us would be available to a being of infinite intellectual powers. There are, however, several problems attached to this form of theological determinism.

One is the problem of maintaining a radical determinism in the face of quantum theory. Has quantum theory not detected a radical unpredictability in the behaviour of particles at a subatomic level? Or is this merely an apparent indeterminacy which is resolved by the operation of variables which at present are hidden from our view. If this is true, the indeterminacy is epistemological only and not ontological. There is no clear consensus on this issue at present. A further problem surrounds human freedom. This may also extend to animal freedom if the cognitive processes of animals also reflect an openness of structure. If God has chosen to endow creatures with freedom, it is possible that this is not a world the precise future of which is determined in advance. In this respect, the conditions under which God has created us result in a voluntary delimiting of divine control and foreknowledge.[36]

A further difficulty concerns the apparent extravagance and profusion in the evolutionary process which we noted at the beginning of this chapter. There are too many blind alleys in the process of evolution, too many extinct species, too much that looks random, fortuitous and experimental for it to resemble a programme every detail of which has been worked out and fixed prior to its commencement.

These problems lead into one of the most formidable issues in modern theology – the action of God upon the world. An examination of the position of one of the leading writers in the current science–religion debate may help us to focus on some of the central options in this field.[37] According to John Polkinghorne, the interplay of chance and necessity enables the creation to change and evolve in fruitful ways. In this respect creation is granted a measure of creaturely independence and freedom. The role of God is one of influence and even interaction, but not in such a way as to override the processes of creation or compromise the integrity of scientific explanation. There is thus an ongoing creativity within the cosmos.

Polkinghorne argues that theology is in search of a model of God's interaction with the world which avoids two errors that have been perpetrated in its history. One is the error of the cosmic tyrant who exercises such a grip on the world that genuine creaturely response is impossible. Here the otherness of the world to God is not granted sufficient scope, and the measure of control exercised by God leads to the depersonalizing of divine–human relations. The other error is that of deism, which consigns God to the role of the indifferent spectator. Having set the universe in motion, God becomes a bystander with neither the power nor the will to become involved in its future progress. A theologically adequate account of God's relationship to the world must construe cosmic history as the unfolding of a world with its own potential and fruitfulness, yet also open to the interaction and ongoing influence of its Maker.

> Because continuous creation allows room for creaturely freedom within this process, the consequences will be lots of things that have come about 'by chance' in the course of history. I do not believe that it was laid down from the foundation of the world that humankind should have five fingers – it has just worked out that way – but I by no means believe that it is pure accident that beings capable of self-consciousness and of worship have emerged in the course of cosmic history. In other words, there is general overall purpose being fulfilled in what is going on, but the details of what actually occurs are left to the contingencies of history (this happening rather than that). The picture is of a world endowed with fruitfulness, guided by its Creator, but allowed an ability to realize this fruitfulness in its own particular ways. Chance is a sign of freedom, not blind purposelessness.[38]

This means that God must be understood as doing more than presiding over the course of the universe, having established the conditions for its open-ended evolution. The action of God must also be seen to be broader than an influence upon the spiritual life of free creatures. This would remove God from the physical dimension of creation, and would have the unintended consequence that God had nothing to do from the big bang until the appearance of the human species on earth. Only a position which accommodates the spontaneity of creation and particular acts of divine providence can make sense both of the modern scientific world view and of much of what Christian faith teaches about the love and patience of God towards creatures. To achieve this, Polkinghorne appeals to models being developed within recent chaos theory.

Chaos theory challenges earlier scientific assumptions that the whole of nature is like a machine that follows patterns which are in principle determined from the outset. This assumption was most famously illustrated by Laplace's comment that to a being of sufficient intellectual power the future would be as fixed and certain as the present. On the basis of a sufficiently comprehensive knowledge of present conditions a super-mind could know everything about the future. We know, however, that phenomena such as the weather or the behaviour of the simplest animal organism cannot be predicted. Small uncertainties become magnified exponentially so that the system within which these function manifests chaotic behaviour. Chaos theory seeks to describe the behaviour of such systems by showing the way in which the constituent elements interact. The behavioural complexity of the system demonstrates how even the smallest fluctuations can yield significant effects at the macro-level. It is this which makes novelty, unpredictability and change features of the history of the cosmos.[39]

Polkinghorne assumes, not uncontroversially, that chaotic systems possess an inherent openness to the future. In other words, unpredictability is not merely a function of human epistemological limitation. It resides within the world itself independently of our cognition. This is not to say that the world evolves and changes in a random and haphazard way. But it is to assume that its future states are in part dependent upon causal principles which are other than the 'bottom-up' descriptions of the interaction between the constituent parts of a system. These causal agencies can be thought of as akin to 'informational input' which determines the context of chaotic systems. This may not only help us to understand how human agents can bring about intentional changes in the physical environment, but also affords a clue as to how God interacts with the cosmos in ways that are scientifically undetectable.[40]

This use of chaos theory is admitted as speculative and tentative. But its theological possibilities make it worthy of consideration. It provides us with a way of understanding God as involved and active in the processes of creation without violating the integrity of their natural order. It seeks consonance between theology and the less deterministic understanding of the world that has come to characterize recent scientific endeavour. It enables us to makes sense of divine action through miracle and special revelation, and also provides some account of the possibilities and limits of petitionary prayer.[41] The Bible portrays God's relationship with creation not merely in terms of preservation but of ongoing struggle and involvement. God's action of sustaining nature relates to the purpose of saving and perfecting the world. Too often we conceive of preservation in static terms as the maintenance of what is already perfect. Yet the Bible speaks frequently of the way in which God is active within the world both in dramatic and in hidden ways: in the career of Joseph at the court of Pharoah (Gen. 45.5); in the victory of Cyrus (Isa. 45.1–7); in the handing over of Jesus to be crucified (Acts 4.24–8).[42]

Before leaving this difficult area, however, we should note a methodological issue. On what basis can we make such a confident affirmation about the providence which governs the evolutionary process? Polkinghorne argues that divine action is undetectable by the instruments and methods of science. The images that he employs to describe this action are self-consciously set within a particular religious context. They are indebted to the Christian tradition and have their source in

convictions about what God has done in the person and work of
Jesus Christ. It is unlikely that one could sustain this world
view simply by deduction from the perceptions of evolutionary
biology. In this respect, one needs to be sceptical about the pro-
spects of a natural theology which deduces conclusions about
the being and purpose of God solely from the data and
theories of modern science. A theology of nature, by contrast,
will seek to offer a theological account of the natural world but
one which is grounded upon convictions regarding divine revelation.[43] It will bring distinctively theological insights to the
conversation with natural science. The pain, toil and extinction
that have marked the history of life make it ambivalent when
viewed from outwith the convictions of a tradition. There is no
natural order of death and resurrection, of sacrifice and redemption, of struggle and successful outcome written into the scientific structure of the cosmos. For the source of this faith one
must look elsewhere.[44]

These two stanzas from Hopkins' 'The Wreck of the *Deutschland*' illustrate this.

I admire thee, master of the tides,
Of the Yore-flood, of the year's fall;
The recurb and the recovery of the gulf's sides,
The girth of it and the wharf of it and the wall;
Stanching, quenching ocean of a motionable mind;
Ground of being, and granite of it: past all
Grasp God, throned behind
Death with a sovereignty that heeds but hides, bodes but abides;

With a mercy that outrides
The all of water, an ark
For the listener; for the lingerer with a love glides
Lower than death and the dark;
A vein for the visiting of the past-prayer, pent in prison,
the-last-breath penitent spirits – the uttermost mark
Our passion-plunged giant risen,
The Christ of the Father compassionate, fetched in the storm
of his strides.

The pattern discerned is one which emerges not through but in spite of natural processes. It comes from the central action of Christ dying and rising, and extends outwards by grace to all of history and nature. The process of creation is known only through the passion of Christ. The outcome of history is secured not by the working out of a process intrinsic to the created realm, but by the re-creative action of God. This point will be developed in the final chapter.

The Animal Creation

A further issue that arises in this context concerns the many species which have become extinct along the evolutionary path. Is their function simply the instrumental one of enabling conscious human beings to emerge at a later date? Are they given a place in the drama of creation only to prepare the way for *Homo sapiens*, the free and conscious creature who can 'glorify God and enjoy him for ever'. Much of the Christian tradition has been unable to think of the significance of animals except in terms of their contribution to human destiny.

Thomas Aquinas argues that three elements determine the moral status of animal life. First, animals are irrational, possessing no mind or reason. Second, they are naturally servile since their end is to serve human beings both by nature and by divine design. Third, they have no moral status in themselves except insofar as they can be considered human property.[45] The extent to which such attitudes were prevalent in the popular treatment of animals has been charted by Keith Thomas in his study *Man and the Natural World*. In seventeenth-century divines for instance one finds prevalent the aforementioned view that animals were created for human welfare. After the Fall animals were less docile than they had been, but in some a natural disposition of obedience to their human masters remains. The instinct which brought shoals of fish to the seashore was a sign that they were intended for human consumption. Animals were placed providentially with human convenience in mind. Camels were allotted to Arabia where there was a shortage of water, and wild beasts were usually sent to deserts where they could do less harm.[46]

Contemporary theology thus provided the moral underpinnings for that ascendancy of man over nature which had by the early modern period become the accepted goal of human endeavour. The dominant religious tradition had no truck with that 'veneration' of nature which many Eastern religions still retained and which the scientist Robert Boyle correctly recognized as 'a discouraging impediment to the empire of man over the inferior creatures'. Since Anglo-Saxon times the Christian Church in England had stood out against the worship of wells and rivers. The pagan divinities of grove, stream and mountain had been expelled, leaving behind them a disenchanted world, to be shaped, moulded and dominated.[47]

The most damaging of all attitudes for the moral status of animals was the Cartesian notion that animals lacked souls and were machines or automata. Animals could thus not even be thought of as sentient; they did not feel pain. The cry of a beaten dog was no more evidence of the brute's suffering than was the sound of an organ proof that the instrument felt pain when struck.[48] However, Thomas goes on to show the gradual shift of attitudes that can be discerned in the eighteenth century. People had for long lived with animals as their daily companions, and were able to communicate with them despite the misgivings of Cartesian philosophers. Dogs and cats came to be accepted as household pets. They were named, fed, cared for, buried and never eaten. A doctrine of animal immortality gradually emerged. The great rationalist theologian Samuel Clarke believed that it was possible that the souls of animals would eventually be resurrected and lodged in Mars, Saturn or some other planet.[49]

We have already seen how there is much scriptural evidence to challenge this humanocentric assumption about the status of animal life. Animals were created before human beings. God takes a delight in them, and the divine providence governs them independent of any reference to human interests. We can see this as confirmed by the history of life on our planet. By comparison with other creatures human beings have emerged only recently. The questions our children ask us are usually the ones with which we have greatest trouble. Why did God create dinosaurs? Will there be pre-historic animals in heaven? We must assume that God takes delight in animal life for its own sake. God takes delight in there being different varieties of sentient creature living, growing and reproducing. The imperfections of the created order do not prevent God's taking pleasure in animals, any more than the imperfections of human existence prevent God valuing us. According to the Old Testament, God offers care to all creatures in the Noahic covenant (Gen. 9.9–17) and values animals which have no obvious human usefulness (Job 39—41).

Though we often overlook it, there is a plethora of references to animals in Scripture, including the Gospels. This is well illustrated by Andrew Linzey in his recent work on *Animal Theology*.

[Jesus'] birth, if tradition is to be believed, takes place in the home of sheep and oxen. His ministry begins, according to Mark, in the wilderness 'with the wild beasts'. His triumphal entry into Jerusalem involves riding on a 'humble ass'. According to Jesus it is lawful to 'do good' on the Sabbath which includes the rescuing of an animal fallen into a pit. Even the sparrows, literally sold for a few pennies in his day, are not 'forgotten before God'. God's providence extends to the entire created order, and the glory of Solomon and all his works cannot be compared to that of the lilies of the field. God so cares for his creation that even 'foxes have holes, and birds of the air have nests; but the Son of man has nowhere to lay his head'.[50]

There is of course a danger of a kind of mawkish sentimentality in our dealings with animals. Much of our behaviour is curiously inconsistent. We educate our children with delightful stories of animals, and teach them to value God's creatures. We are fascinated by David Attenborough's commentaries on wildlife and by Rolf Harris's animal surgery. Yet for much of the time we turn a blind eye to the conditions under which animals are bred, fed, housed and slaughtered before their flesh ends up on our supermarket shelves. Peter Singer has pointed out that for most urban dwellers the main contact with other species is at meal times: we eat them.[51]

The ethical status of animals has been widely debated only in recent years. Much of the literature suggests that our attitudes to animals are gravely disordered. It is argued that whatever reasons we have for treating other human beings with respect must apply *mutatis mutandis* also to animals. If human beings are of inherent value, then so are animals. If the suffering of human beings should be prevented then so should that of animals. If human beings can experience pleasure and the enjoyment of life, then so can animals. At the same time, it can be pointed out that arguments which distinguish human beings as unique by virtue of their reason or autonomy frequently break down when applied to infants or those suffering from senile dementia. We should not use these criteria to exclude either some human beings or all non-human animals.

One of the difficulties of the debate surrounding animal welfare is that much of the discourse is conducted in terms of rights. This is problematic, partly because it is not clear what we mean by human rights. Some philosophers have argued that rights language only makes sense in the context of correlative notions of exercising, enjoying, claiming, asserting, waiving rights and so on. In this sense only persons can be the bearers of rights. It is not intelligible to speak about animals, trees, plants, or material objects possessing rights. They are not members of communities which have rights. The newly born, the enfeebled and the comatose may by extension be thought of as rights holders since their inability to exercise or waive rights is a temporary or contingent matter.[52] But animals cannot be thus included within the moral community. Thus we have a fundamental disagreement between those who do and those who do not believe in animal rights.

In this context, the theology of creation may have something to contribute. It is possible to avoid altogether the quasi-legal discourse of human rights and to understand why from the perspective of the Creator animals may have value. They are an integral feature of the good creation which God has called into being. They are a source of delight to their Maker. Human beings are created in an environment in which other animals already exist and are given responsibilities in relation to them. The eschatological vision of the Old Testament is one in which the different species co-exist in peace and harmony. In this connection Stanley Hauerwas and John Berkman have remarked that vegetarianism may be an appropriate form of Christian eschatological witness.[53]

To value animals for the life that God has bestowed upon them is one way of countering humanocentric tendencies in theology.[54] It is an imperative which has gained growing recognition in the churches. The need to maintain the integrity of creation and protect the life of all the world is a leading theme of the reports of the World Council of Churches' commission on Justice, Peace and the Integrity of Creation. The following guidelines were set out for Christian action in a special WCC report commissioned in 1988.

> i. Avoid cosmetics and household products that have been cruelly tested on animals. Instead, buy cruelty-free items. ii. Avoid clothing and other aspects of fashion that have a history of cruelty to animals, products of the fur industry in particular. Instead, purchase clothes that are cruelty-free. iii. Avoid meat and animal products that have been produced on factory farms. Instead, purchase meats and animals products from sources where animals have been treated with respect, or abstain from these products altogether. iv. Avoid patronizing forms of entertainment that treat animals as mere means to human ends. Instead, seek benign forms of entertainment, ones that nurture a sense of the wonder of God's creation and reawaken that duty of conviviality we can discharge by living respectfully in community with all life, the animals included.[55]

Value is to be attached to created things not simply because of their instrumental usefulness for human beings. What God has created can be of value to God prior to and independently of any human concerns. Yet to attach ethical significance to all forms of life, however, does not necessarily imply the position of biotic egalitarianism. This is the view that all living creatures are worthy of equal moral respect. It is akin to Albert Schweitzer's principle of 'reverence for life' and to some trends in deep ecology. Thus the insect becomes of equal value to the chimpanzee. This position can easily lead to absurdity, and needs to be countered with some gradation of value which can make moral distinctions between different species. To claim that all creatures are worthy of moral consideration is not to say that they are of equal moral significance. In this respect, there is a case for perceiving some hierarchy of species which enables us to perceive some as more capable of realizing and bearing values than others. Process theology is instructive in this respect. Charles Birch argues that if we think in terms of richness of experience as enabled by the development of the central nervous system we can view primates and whales as of greater intrinsic worth than worms and mosquitoes. 'I have no difficulty in applauding the campaign of the World Worldlife Fund to save the chimpanzees of Africa. Nor have I difficulty in applauding the campaign of the World Health Organization to eradicate the smallpox virus and the malarial parasite.'[56]

There are two difficulties with this gradation of value when applied to environmental activity. First, it ignores the important contribution made to ecosystems by insects and bacteria nearer the bottom end of the hierarchy. Thus, the environment may suffer far greater destruction through failure to protect a species of insect than through the extinction of a species of mammal. This insight clearly needs to be accommodated within environmental ethics. The instrumental value of a species in its contribution to the biosphere cannot be ignored. Nonetheless, graded rankings seem inevitable in tough decisions that have to be taken involving life-forms in conflict situations.[57]

A second problem concerns the implicit humanocentrism in a hierarchy which appears to place human beings at the top of the evolutionary tree. Is this simply a way of perceiving the world as having a moral bias in favour of the human species?[58] This objection notwithstanding, it is difficult to avoid taking some such decision in cases of conflict. Such decisions will involve an implicit gradation of value. Do we allow a human being to perish if the only form of treatment for her heart condition involves transplanting an organ from a pig? The uniqueness of human beings seems integral to much of the Christian tradition. It is difficult to gainsay this. Human beings alone are created in the image of God even if they share much in common with other creatures. The covenant God makes is with human beings even if the rest of creation is thereby represented. Jesus Christ became incarnate as a human being even if as flesh and blood he shares in our animal existence. It ought to be possible to value all animals for their own sakes while at the same time providing a sober account of what is unique about human beings. This need not carry the implication that the evolutionary process is set up with the single intention of producing human beings. We have a central place in God's creation but not an exclusive one.

One problem to be faced here is the size and age of the universe. It is incredibly old and large, so why should we assign to ourselves a central place in the story of creation. One answer is to point to the way in which it takes a universe like ours an awful lot of time and space to produce conscious life. Another response is to point out that if significance is measured by complexity of structure and consciousness then the emergence of human life is indeed remarkable. Ian Barbour has pointed out that

> the greatest complexity has apparently been achieved in the middle range of size, not at atomic dimensions or galactic dimensions. There are a hundred trillion synapses in a human brain; the number of possible ways of connecting them is greater than the number of atoms in the universe. A higher level of organisation and a greater richness of experience occurs in a human being than in a thousand lifeless galaxies. It is human beings, after all, that reach out to understand that cosmic immensity.[19]

Evolutionary theory is able to point to the way in which we are very much part of the natural world. At the same time, it reveals that nature has produced some strikingly new forms of life in us. This makes sense in light of our earlier reading of Genesis 1—2. Adam belongs to the natural world and is created from the dust. In terms of our bodily functions and disorders we share much in common with our animal kindred. The convergence of much research work in veterinary and human medicine bears recent testimony to this. Yet in manifesting the image of God, Adam is distinguished by capacity from other creatures. We know that African chimpanzees and gorillas share about 99 per cent of their DNA with human beings, but the 1 per cent difference makes for some striking changes in forms of life.[60] Chimpanzees can be taught to communicate in signs but are not fully capable of language. Research suggests that chimpanzees may be capable of abstract thought, but even this is still far below the level of an average two-year-old child.

Higher animals have some forms of self-awareness but not the level of self-consciousness we find in human beings. We have a greater capacity for memory, for envisioning the future and for the manipulation of linguistic symbols to abstract from the immediate present. We can reflect on the purpose of human existence, ponder our finitude and create works of art which afford new horizons of meaning. In our social and linguistic life (since Wittgenstein we cannot separate these) we thus display a far greater complexity than other creatures. Insects and dolphins have social orders for mating, rearing and instructing offspring, and for feeding and protecting the group. But human beings have books, the media, systems of education and entertainment. Human intellectual power and creativity make rational discrimination possible. This realizes the possibility of a cultural tradition which is relatively independent of considerations of natural selection. The human being is a point of convergence between two streams of information; one is inherited and genetic while the other is cultural.[61] As carriers of cultural information, human beings introduce new possibilities and forms of freedom to the created order. Thus the human mind is capable of rational evaluation, aesthetic appreciation, and moral perception which are not directly linked to criteria of fitness for survival. Our intellectual development enables us to judge what is beautiful, good and true over and above the demands of natural selection. That this possibility has been created by evolutionary progress does not mean that it is explicable purely in biological terms. This point is well made by John Bowker in his recent criticism of the reductionist tendencies of sociobiology. The mind may value what is good, true and beautiful irrespective of its survival value. There thus emerges a history of cultural transmission which demands to be assessed in terms other than those of evolutionary biology.[62] It is now possible for cultural evolution explicitly to counteract the course of physical evolution. Even Richard Dawkins has commended the welfare state for being unnatural in the protection it affords the weak and the unfit. It overrides the impulse of the selfish gene. Though unnatural, he describes it as a crowning glory of human achievement. In a similar vein, Gerd Theissen illustrates how the teaching of Jesus contests the drift of natural selection. By introducing new possibilities our biological nature is both redeemed and fulfilled. He praises those who castrate themselves for the kingdom of heaven (Matt. 19.10–12). He urges his followers to recognize a higher loyalty than that of family and home (Luke 14.26). The love of neighbour is to be extended even to those who belong to groups with which we are at enmity (Luke 10.29–37).[63]

The emergence of cultural evolution in which persons can discriminate freely between truth and falsehood, and can raise the fundamental questions of life, is of considerable theological significance. It provides the conditions within which divine revelation can take place through prophets, precepts and the history of a people. The preoccupation of theology, therefore, with events that have taken place only over the last three millennia makes some sense. On the other hand, one cannot allow this insight to promote an easy evolutionary optimism. The process of selection, by its very nature, entails that there are innumerable losers as well as winners in the evolution of life. Soteriology must therefore be understand not in terms of the revelation of an inherent dynamic within the process of life. It must be seen as a reordering and redeeming of all that has been destroyed, wasted and lost in natural as well as social history. In his recent work, Moltmann has sought to locate the cosmic christology of the New Testament in this evolutionary context.[64] The Christ of Ephesians and Colossians is the one through whom all things are created and in whom all things find their appointed end. This means that his coming in glory is accompanied by a transformation of the whole of nature. This is not a realization of immanent natural forces, *pace* Teilhard de Chardin and Karl Rahner, but a divine transfiguring of the cosmos intimated in the resurrection of Jesus from the dead. Christ must therefore be confessed as the One who, with the Father and the Spirit, redeems evolution. In the final chapter, we shall consider the problem of evil and the question of the end of created life.

CHAPTER FOUR

Creation, Evil and the End of Life

The Limits of Theodicy

The greatest difficulty facing any theology of creation is to provide an account of evil. The love and power of God raise the question of why natural and moral evil are permitted to exist in such excessive quantities in the created universe. Natural evil includes the suffering that arises for human beings and other animals from such phenomena as famine, flood, earthquake and disease. Moral evil typically refers to the suffering that is brought about by human malevolence. Like natural evil it takes many forms which include persecution, hatred, murder and rape. It is evil for which we are culpable. The ancient problem facing Christian belief was presented by David Hume in the form of a simple dilemma. 'Epicurus' old questions are yet unanswered. Is he willing to prevent evil, but not able? then is he impotent. Is he able but not willing? then is he malevolent. Is he both able and willing? whence then is evil?'[1] The task of theodicy is the formidable one of justifying God in the presence of evil.

In the history of the tradition theologians were once able to reconcile the goodness of God with the perfection of the original creation by appeal to the doctrine of the Fall. We should not underestimate the significance of this doctrine and its hold over the popular Christian imagination, at least in the Latin West. It enabled theology to affirm the goodness of the created order while also giving an adequate account of its present state of turmoil. The explanation and blame for this could be laid at the door of Adam and in him all humanity. The moral disorder of the human species was a consequence of

Adam's fall from grace. The physical disorder of the cosmos, moreover, was as a result of demonic influence within a creation which had been set on the wrong trajectory by the first human couple. We can see all this graphically set out in Augustine's *City of God*. Evil is not inherent in the original structure of the universe. It is described negatively in terms of the falling away from goodness of free rational creatures, whether angelic or human. Natural evil is explained in terms of the effects of moral evil. This feature of Augustine's fall doctrine is of enormous importance to his theodicy, and we should not underestimate its significance for his doctrine of evil.

> This present life of ours is evidence that all the mortal descendants of the first man came under condemnation ... [T]here are the fear of the dreadful calamities from non-human sources; and they are past counting: the dread of the extremes of heat and cold; of storm tempest, and flood; of thunder and lightning, hail and thunderbolt; of earthquakes and upheavals; the terror of being crushed by falling buildings; of attacks by animals, in panic or in malice; of the bites of wild beasts, which may only be painful, but may sometimes be fatal ... Again, there are the evils that arise from the body, in the shape of diseases; and there are so many of them all the books of physicians cannot contain them all. And in many of those, indeed in almost all of them, the treatments and the medicines are themselves instruments of torture, so that patients are rescued from a painful end by a painful cure.[2]

N. P. Williams pointed out in his Bampton Lectures on original sin and the Fall that the most significant function of these doctrines in the early Church was their theodicial function. In other words, the Fall could explain why what was originally the good creation was now in a state of corruption. From Origen onwards theologians were able to resolve the problem of evil in large measure by appeal to the effects of original sin. 'Origen grasped the all-important principle that the Fall-doctrine really rests upon an inference from the phenomena of evil considered in the light of ethical monotheism, and not upon the Paradise narrative of Genesis III.'[3]

Whatever one makes of the Fall doctrine as historical explanation, particularly of natural evil, one should not ignore its abiding value as phenomenological description. It continues to function as a necessary description of the universal reality of sin both as an inherited condition and as a climate into which we are born. The difficulties with the doctrine, to which we shall come, should not prevent us from seeing this. One of the best recent accounts of this subject is Cornelius Plantinga's *Not the Way It's Supposed to Be: A Breviary of Sin*. There Plantinga offers a Christian phenomenology of sin which shows that we do not understand our condition adequately without recourse to the categories that theology has employed to describe sin. He shows, moreover, that unless we can recapture the discourse of sin, the related discourse of Christ as Saviour and the forgiveness of sins will sound quaint. Through countless illustrations from literature and contemporary life he describes how the vocabulary of sin is necessary to make sense of what we are and how we act. As a subtle and illuminating description of sin this is one of the best.

We must speak of the 'universality, solidarity, stubbornness, and historical momentum of sin'.[4] The sins we typically manifest are not simply of our own making but issue from traditions of prejudice, skewed perception and disordered desire. At the same time sin must be understood not merely as moral wrongdoing but as a departure from the true end of life, a declension in which we fail to become the people that God wishes us to be.

> The point of our lives is not to get smart or to get rich or even to get happy. The point is to discover God's purposes for us and to make them our own. The point is to learn ways of loving God above all and our neighbours as ourselves and then to use these loves the way a golfer uses checkpoints to set up for a drive. The point is to be lined up right, to seek first the kingdom of God, to try above all to increase the net amount of shalom in the world.[5]

Sin is essentially negative in character. It is parasitic upon things that can be considered good. Even Satan's virtues are largely traditional. Sin vandalizes and spoils what is otherwise worthy. 'Sinful life is a partly depressing, partly ludicrous caricature of genuine human life.'[6]

Although the doctrine of sin is still necessary to make sense of who we are as human creatures before God, its theodicial function has nonetheless been seriously disturbed by modern science. The central difficulty in using original sin to explain the intrusion of evil into the created order is that the causes of natural evil predate the emergence of the human species. Created life was characterized by suffering, disease, struggle and death before the appearance of human beings on our planet. To attribute these phenomena to the original sin of our first ancestors is now impossible. While the doctrine of sin may continue to provide a necessary description of our situation it does not provide an explanation of the cause of natural evil; of earthquakes, famines, flood, disease and death. This problem was illustrated for me by a geologist who pointed to the existence of fossils which reveal that dinosaurs died riddled with the most painful forms of arthritis. Disease, suffering and death were thus present in the created order long before the appearance of human beings. Our ancestors found themselves sharing in the lot of created life everywhere on our planet. The notion that their condition was originally perfect, their first sin bringing about disastrous changes to the cosmic environment, is now untenable. However much natural evil has been compounded by human sin, one cannot make any simple cause–effect correlation. Thus John Polkinghorne, whose theological instincts are generally orthodox, has written bluntly of his difficulties with the doctrine of the Fall. Death was always present within the animal world from which the human species evolved. We can detect no discontinuity in the course of natural history, no signs of a golden age from which the creation declined.[7]

The problem of theodicy is felt more acutely by theologians in the late twentieth century than at any previous period in the history of theology. This of course is not to say that earlier thinkers have not reflected on evil with as much profundity as modern ones. But the widespread unease surrounding theolo-

gies of evil is indicated today by the way in which the very enterprise of theodicy has been called into question as theologically
misplaced and morally inappropriate.

The standard moves of theodicy do not need to be rehearsed.
There are arguments with a measure of validity which claim
that suffering is an inevitable by-product of a world in which
creatures are free, in which life has to evolve through struggle,
and in which human beings have to acquire virtues of courage,
generosity, self-discipline and perseverance. One might distinguish three possible moves that have been made by theologians
and philosophers over the centuries.[8] The free-will defence
argues that human freedom is a necessary and desirable feature
of a worthwhile human life. Yet, the price of free will is that
human beings will have the ability to inflict evil upon one
another and the rest of creation. The instrumental theodicy
claims that a measure of suffering and harshness in our environment are necessary if we are to develop those virtues which
God wills for us. A world in which there is natural evil will
thus elicit responses of perseverance, courage, sacrifice and generosity which cannot otherwise be realized. 'We need those insi-
dious processes of decay and dissolution which money and
strength cannot ward off for long', says Swinburne, 'to give us
the opportunities, so easy otherwise to avoid, to become
heroes.'[9] Finally, a world which contains some darkness,
shadow and dissonance may be one whose harmony is all the
more moving and majestic. This view is expressed by Plotinus,
who claims that the graded succession of life-forms is an expression of a Reason replete with intellectual variety.

We are like people ignorant of painting who complain that the
colours are not beautiful everywhere in the picture; but the
Artist has laid on the appropriate tint to every spot. Note also
that cities, however well governed, are not composed of
citizens who are all equal. Again, we are censuring a drama
because the persons are not all heroes but include a servant and
a rustic and some scurrilous clown; yet take away the low charac-
ters and the power of the drama is gone; these are part and
parcel of it.[10]

Yet the overriding difficulty that accounts such as this face is that they cannot accommodate the excess of evil we see all around us. What seems like a sensible apologetic proposal melts away when confronted with burning questions about the quantity and depth of evil in the cosmos. Since Dostoevsky's tirade in the mouth of Ivan Karamazov we have become forever attuned to the question 'what about the children?' Ivan after describing the most awful abuse of a child by her parents has this to say to his brother Alyosha, a novice monk.

[This poor child of five was subjected to every possible torture by those cultivated parents. They beat her, thrashed her, kicked her for no reason till her body was one bruise. Then they went to greater refinements of cruelty – shut her up all night in the cold and frost in a privy, and because she didn't ask to be taken at night (as though a child of five sleeping its angelic, sound sleep could be trained to wake and ask), they smeared her face and filled her mouth with excrement, and it was her mother, her mother, did this! And that mother could sleep, hearing the poor child's groans!] Can you understand why a little creature, who can't even understand what's done to her, should beat her little aching heart with her tiny fist in the dark and the cold, and weep her meek unresentful tears to dear, kind God to protect her? Do you understand that, friend and brother, you pious and humble novice? Do you understand why this infamy must be and is permitted? Without it, I am told, man could not have existed on earth, for he could not have known good and evil. Why should he know that diabolical good and evil when it costs so much? Why, the whole world of knowledge is not worth that child's prayer to 'dear, kind God!'. I say nothing of the sufferings of grown-up people, they have eaten the apple, damn them, and the devil take them all! But these little ones![11]

One can find other equally graphic examples from recent literature which expose the shortcomings of any traditional theodicy. Elie Wiesel's description of the slow death of a boy by hanging before thousands of fellow inmates and members of the SS at Buna, near Auschwitz, or William Styron's account of the choice imposed upon Sophie when she is told to choose which of her children is to be gassed and which is to be spared. 'I can't choose! I can't choose! She began to scream. Oh, how she recalled her own screams! Tormented angels never screeched so loudly above hell's pandemonium. "Ich kann nicht wählen!" she screamed.'[12]

In the face of such atrocities it is sometimes said that theodicy is morally corrupting. To justify a world in which such things occur is to compromise one's ethical sensibilities. Theodicy attempts to justify the unjustifiable. In softening the outrage, it weakens our resolve to combat evil wherever we encounter it. By insisting that everything is for the best, theodicy distorts our moral perception and response to evil in all its manifestations. A more adequate theological response, it is said, must seek not to justify but to assist every initiative for overcoming suffering and resisting evil.[13] The only justifiable response is one of protest.

Where protest theodicy and the theology of the cross have become aligned is in the recognition that the God of Jesus stands not apart from but within the predicament of suffering. By identifying with those who are victims of evil, God is positioned with those who suffer against the forces that cause their suffering. In this voluntary identification with every victim and every sinner, the protest against evil is intensified, and the eschatological hope is offered that this is not the way things will finally be. A theological response to evil therefore seeks not to explain why it has come about but looks forward *per crucem* to its final defeat in the Kingdom of God. There are strong scriptural grounds for asserting that the Christian faith's prime interest should be in proclaiming the defeat of evil rather than in seeking its explanation. 'On that day the Lord with his cruel and great and strong sword will punish Leviathan the twisting serpent, and he will kill the dragon that is in the sea' (Isa. 27.1).

However, where problems arise with this approach is in the doctrine of creation. Protest theodicy and some recent theologies of the cross could make good sense of a Marcionite distinction between the God of creation and the God of redemption. It is said that Donald MacKinnon used to remark in his lectures, 'If I am to be arraigned for heresy, then let it be Manichaeism.' There is some Christian sense in this utterance. God's work is in the defeat of the evil endemic to the created order. God is involved in the protest at the way things are and is working towards their abolition. All this is right. Yet the doctrine of creation teaches that the redeeming God is also the sovereign creator.

No theory will justify the excessive quantity of evil and none will be appropriate as a pastoral response, but some attempt needs to be made to describe the way in which the creation despite its beauty and magnificent order is so imperfect. Perhaps one might invoke here a distinction between describing and justifying. To describe the circumstances under which an agent has performed a particular action is not to justify that action. A description which helps us to understand why something has come about is not equivalent to its moral justification. A description of evil will situate it within the creative and redemptive purpose of God without the assumption that this can function as an adequate explanation which resolves the problem of evil.

It is significant that Moltmann, who is so adamant that there can be no justification of the sufferings of the innocent, attempts something very like such a description of evil when he comes to the doctrine of creation out of nothing. At the very least, the theology of creation has to attempt some description of evil which is consonant with its Christian convictions about the goodness of God and the creative process. Treatments of the kenotic aspect of creation which mesh with more traditional theodicies may have something to say in this context. The conditions of creating a world fit for the divine purpose are those conditions which give rise to moral and natural evil. We find recourse to this argument in the work of a wide range of theologians. For example, Brunner writes of God's voluntary self-limitation in creation. The glory of God is manifested in the response of free creatures to God's Word of love. To do this God imposes upon the divine self a large measure of self-limitation. This he describes as a *kenosis*, a self-emptying which creates the possibility that creaturely freedom will be used to defy God. 'The kenosis, which reaches its paradoxical climax in the Cross of Christ, began with the Creation of the world.'[14]

Recent science has also contributed to this description of evil. In God's providing a contingent creation with a stable and evolving life in which conscious beings can emerge for covenantal relation, there is a risk undertaken. There is a voluntary renunciation of a particular type of control.[15] The creation is one which is allowed to evolve according to the interplay of chance and necessity. Its emergence in its present form is willed by God not in the sense that everything that happens is desired by God but in the sense that creation is permitted to become in this way. Yet this is not a divine stand-off. It is not the withdrawal of a spectator but rather the relinquishing of control that is appropriate to a particular type of agency. God's action is one in which the creation is redeemed from within rather than overruled from without. This letting-be of the world is itself an act of costly love which is consonant with the cost of redemption by the crucifixion of Christ. Simone Weil once wrote, 'Because he is the creator God is not all-powerful. Creation is abdication. But he is all-powerful in this sense, that his abdication is voluntary. He knows its effects and wills them. . . . God has emptied himself. This means that both the Creation and the Incarnation are included with the Passion.'[16] The difference between this view and a similar view found in process theology is that God's letting-be of creation is the result of an act of voluntary self-abdication. It is a voluntary self-abdication which already has in view an eschatological goal.[17]

Hopkins' 'Wreck of the *Deutschland*' was a poem written on the occasion of the death of five German nuns when a vessel, the *Deutschland*, hit a sand bank at the mouth of the Thames in a midwinter storm. He read of the incident in *The Times* on 11 December 1875. 'Five German nuns, whose bodies are now in the dead-house here, clasped hands and were drowned together, the chief sister, a gaunt woman 6ft high, calling out loudly and often "O Christ, come quickly!" till the end came. The shrieks and sobbing of women and children are described by the survivors as agonising.'

Hopkins was haunted by this account and was shamed by the

further discovery that the German nuns had come to Britain seeking political asylum only to be turned away by the authorities.[18] It took him six months to write the poem, and was his first great effort after a silence of seven years. Critics have argued that it is a flawed poem both theologically and aesthetically: it is too elaborate and wordy; it is drenched in sexual imagery; it is occasionally sentimental and loses sight of the particular suffering and death it describes; it attacks the Reformation with sectarian loathing; and it pins too much on the symbol of the tall, drowning German nun. Nonetheless, it is a poem which has much to say about the grandeur of the world, the depths of suffering and the goal of all life as redeemed by the passion of Christ. It bears witness to the glory of the Creator but tells us that God's sovereignty though it heeds is also hidden. It is hidden for two reasons which concern the corruption of creation and the veiling of the Creator in Christ. For Hopkins the person of Jesus is not merely an expression of the Logos which is known everywhere as the indwelling principle of creation. Since Christ is of the substance of the Father – since Sonship is of the eternal essence of God – the indwelling principle of creation can only be identified by reference to Christ's incarnation and passion. In this respect, Christ is not merely an expression of the Creator. Creation itself is Christ-shaped and centred.[19]

The sense of the hiddenness of God was intensified in Hopkins' later poetry, especially *The Terrible Sonnets* of 1885. Paul Fiddes in a theological analysis of these poems suggests that Hopkins did not so much suffer a loss of faith as come to the realization that the incarnate Christ was hidden in the pain and misery of the world. 'If Christ is no longer celebrated as shining out in the wildfire of nature, this is not because he is absent but because he is hidden in the ashes and clinkers.'[20] Thus Hopkins writes of the resurrection in what some critics consider to be his greatest poem.

> Enough! the Resurrection,
> A heart's clarion! Away grief's gasping, joyless days, dejection.
> Across my foundering deck shone
> A beacon, an eternal beam. Flesh fade, and mortal trash

Fall to the residuary worm: world's wildfire, leave but ash:
In a flash, at a trumpet crash,
I am all at once what Christ is, since he was what I am, and
This Jack, joke, poor potsherd, patch, matchwood,
    immortal diamond,
Is immortal diamond.[21]

Creation can only be understood from the perspective of redemption. There is too much wastage, pain and untimely death to make this view possible apart from a particular conviction about the meaning of Christ's death and resurrection. Yet the resurrection takes place within the context of Jewish hopes about the general resurrection from the dead, the coming of the kingdom, and the establishment of God's righteousness. In this way the understanding of the ways of God in creation already looks toward the end of all things. This brings us to the subject of eschatology.

Scientific Eschatology

In Chapter One we noted how scriptural references to creation were often bound up with hopes for the future. What God had once done in bringing the world into being can only be comprehended by reference to the promised future. The idea of continuous creation gives expression to the idea that God continues to make the world according to a purpose that is in view. Recent scientific eschatologies, however, raise some pertinent questions for theology. We have enquired into the significance of the vast age of the universe, but what about the vastness of its future? With the realization that we live in an expanding universe, there has arisen the question of whether the expansion will continue indefinitely or whether the universe will eventually contract. We now have books not only on the first three minutes but also on the last three minutes.[22] These two possibilities give rise to two very different scenarios. One is the so-called big crunch of the closed universe in which the expansion halts, with matter steadily contracting to implode upon itself. The other scenario is the heat death of an open universe in which the expansion continues but as stars burn out there is the eventual dissolution of galaxies into enormous black holes. Scientists appear to be divided on the question of which scenario is the more likely. Much depends on the amount of matter in the universe. Is there enough to reverse expansion and thus bring about contraction? Or is the amount of matter less than that required to prevent indefinite expansion? Either way it is difficult on the basis of modern cosmology to be optimistic about the ultimate future of the universe. This places a final question mark against any belief in evolutionary optimism.[23] In a famous passage, Bertrand Russell once commented on the implications of the heat-death of the universe. 'All the labour of the ages, all the devotion, all the inspiration, all the noonday brightness of human genius, are destined to extinction in the vast death of the solar system ... [A]ll these things, if not quite beyond dispute, are yet so nearly certain that no philosophy which rejects them can hope to stand. Only within the scaffolding of these truths, only on the firm foundation of unyielding despair, can the soul's habitation henceforth be safely built.'[24]

A plea for greater attention to the questions raised by scientific prognoses for the universe has been made by Wolfhart Pannenberg in the context of the dialogue between science and religion. He asks how Christian statements about the coming end of the world can be reconciled with scientific theories which predict a future that will last for billions of years. The scientific prediction that the conditions to sustain life will last for far longer than conscious life has yet been around is hard to relate to the urgency with which the Bible speaks of the end of history.[25]

Nonetheless, recent attempts have been made to sketch scientific eschatologies which offer hope in the face of this eventual cosmic catastrophe.[26] Freeman Dyson suggests that in an open universe human beings might learn to adapt to conditions very different from those we presently enjoy. This will be the supreme test of the adaptability of life in about 10^{33} years from now. In his Gifford Lectures, Dyson suggests that through human initiative life will eventually be exported to other planets and galaxies. This life will have to be able to survive in conditions of zero-gravity, zero-temperature and zero-pressure. The last condition, zero-pressure, is the most troublesome, but Dyson predicts that just as life moved from water to air half a billion years ago, so it can make a similar transition from air to vacuum.[27]

He goes on to consider the even larger question of the future of life in an open cosmos that proceeds towards death by slow freezing rather than quick frying. The nature of life, he claims, resides in organization rather than substance. Consciousness is the result of a particular form of organization and could therefore be reproduced in forms detached from flesh and blood. Thus intelligence could become embodied 'in networks of superconducting circuitry or in interstellar dust clouds'.[28] As the universe grows progressively colder, life can adapt by matching its metabolism of energy to the falling temperature. If we assume the adaptability of life, the rate of energy will fall with the square of the environmental temperature. In an infinitely expanding universe, he concludes, life can survive on a finite store of energy.[29]

Another attempt to offer a more hopeful vision of the future is worked out by Frank Tipler in his highly popular book, *The Physics of Immortality*. Tipler favours the hypothesis of the closed universe of the big crunch. He believes that physics can provide a solution to many ancient theological problems, and he complains that most theologians today are largely ignorant of eschatology. The time has come, he says, 'to absorb theology into physics, to make Heaven as real as an electron'.[30] Like Dyson's proposal, Tipler's response is predicated on the view that the human mind is a software programme within the hardware of the brain. This program could conceivably be transferred to other hardware. In the final phase of a collapsing universe vast amounts of energy would be available. By manipulating the uneven collapse rate of the universe, life can harness sufficient energy to survive and prosper. It can do this to the nth degree at an Omega Point made possible by the conditions prior to the big crunch. Here life is able to control all matter and energy states, and can gather sufficient energy for an infinite amount of information-processing. To the consciousness processing the information this amounts to an infinite subjective time, even though there is only a finite period of time between the attainment of the Omega Point and the final singularity. The Omega Point becomes for Tipler omnipresent, omniscient and infinite.

Immortality is achieved by virtue of an emulation of the entire physical universe at the Omega Point. The information-processing power achieved at this point can emulate all possible quantum states for every possible being. With the emulation of the cells, molecules, atoms and sub-atomic particles which make the people who were, are and will be, we are all effectively resurrected at this Omega Point.[31]

> It is a logically necessary consequence of eternal progress that our species become extinct. For we are finite beings, we have definite limits. Our brains can code only so much information, we can understand only rather simple arguments. If the ascent of life into the Omega Point is to occur, one day the most advanced minds must be non-Homo sapiens. ... Since the universal computer capacity increases without bound as the Omega Point is approached, it follows that, if only a bare bones description of our current world is stored permanently, then there will inevitably come a time when there will be sufficient computer capacity to simulate our present-day world by simple brute force: by creating an exact simulation – an emulation – of all logically possible variants of our world.[32]

The obvious difficulty with the eschatologies of both Dyson and Tipler is in their speculative nature. Even a non-specialist can quickly discern the level of conjecture and fantasy involved in these visions of the future. In particular, the problems involved in harnessing cosmic energy in the run-in to the big crunch must be formidable. Paul Davies in his recent contribution to the debate has suggested that the quantum effects of the final gravitational collapse of matter may well set a limit to the rate of information-processing. 'If so,' he says, 'let us hope that the cosmic superbeing or supercomputer will at least come to understand existence well enough in the available time to become reconciled to its own mortality.'[33]

On the other hand, exponents of these scientific eschatologies can point to the time that human intelligence has to work out the details and overcome the immense difficulties of bringing about such a state of affairs. If we have hundreds of billion years left to us then why be pessimistic about a few practical details? One might respond, however, that the more immediate nuclear and ecological problems we face are a greater threat to our extinction.

From a theological perspective, several issues arise. It is questionable whether this type of scenario in any way constitutes an eschatological fulfilment. It is a long way from Isaiah's image of a redeemed community of creation in which the wolf shall dwell with the lamb, and a little child shall lead them (Isa. 11). Biblical images of the eschatological community construe redeemed life as social and embodied. The person is not to be reduced to the mind as information-processing software. Too much of what makes us distinctively human is lost by construing the essential self as an information carrier. In any event, Tipler's theory of immortality faces the formidable philosophical criticism that his resurrected persons are no more than replicas of those who have once lived. As replicas they cannot be identical to those they emulate so perfectly.

One suspects, however, that with increasing attention being devoted to artificial intelligence, we shall see further attempts to work out eschatologies of information-processing and virtual reality. This calls for greater attention to the question of what it means to be a person. In this regard Fergus Kerr has made a timely warning against what he calls 'the new Cartesianism' of artificial intelligence. This is a new version of an old story in which human beings envision their intellectual nature as functioning better outwith the body and beyond the normal constraints of space and time. 'The desire to think away our incarnate nature remains as seductive as ever in our culture.'[34]

A second problem is that theological eschatology is not exclusively concerned with the final state of our physical universe, any more than the doctrine of creation is exclusively concerned with its initial state. Eschatology determines all of life wherever and whenever it has been lived. It involves all of God's creatures and not only those who are present at the end of the world. This was traditionally expressed by apocalyptic images of the tombs being opened and the dead awakened on the last day. The destiny of creation is one in which all who have ever lived are caught up. The omega point envisaged by Tipler is one in which all information is reproduced, but this is hardly a hope that is likely to enliven us here and now billions of years in advance. The rather chilling science fiction world of physical eschatology is not calculated to inspire confidence in the long-term future of intelligent life. Thus it is no surprise to find Polkinghorne remarking, 'I regard physical eschatology as presenting us with the ultimate *reductio ad absurdum* of a merely evolutionary optimism.'[35] We are a long way from the hope expressed in the credal confession of the communion of the saints as a reality in which we already share, and in the eucharistic prayer for the union of the Church on earth with the Church in heaven.

It is important also to delineate the relationship of eschatology to evolution. Christian convictions about the outcome of life are based not on prognostications about the end state of the evolution of life within the cosmos. Apart from the difficulties that this entails for all those who have been sacrificed along the way, it is hard to discern any unitary teleology on a cosmic scale. It is more appropriate, therefore, to conceive of eschatology in terms of God's re-creation and reconfiguring of entities, events and processes which have emerged and disappeared throughout the history of the universe. This reconstitutive work of God may thus embrace species which have already become extinct, as well as human beings facing the prospect of extinction through either their own folly or ineluctable cosmic processes. Thus Keith Ward argues that '[i]mmortality for animals as well as humans, is a necessary condition of any acceptable theodicy'.[36]

Biblical Eschatology

Biblical eschatology in its wider sense is dominated by both prophetic and apocalyptic expectations. Much of prophetic expectation is directed towards the future history of Israel and the history of the world. It holds out the promise of an improvement in the nation's fortunes based upon the grace of God which calls for a response of human obedience. Within apocalyptic literature, however, the final fulfilment of creation is seen as dependent upon the irruption of God into the flow of world history. There is thus a more radical discontinuity between present time and the future age. The promise of the latter is dependent upon the action of the sovereign God. There is no natural evolutionary progression from the present to the promised future.

This tension between prophetic expectation and apocalyptic hope is worked out in the New Testament and the Christian tradition. In the teaching of Jesus people are confronted with a decision that is of eschatological significance. 'The time is fulfilled, and the kingdom of God has come near; repent and believe in the good news' (Mark 1.15). Here the present has taken on decisive significance by virtue of a future that is already breaking in. Jesus' resurrection from the dead, and his presence in the Church through the Holy Spirit, are to be understood in terms of their eschatological significance. The resurrection is the sign and guarantee of the general resurrection of the dead; the Christian life in the Spirit is already the first fruit of a coming kingdom. This life in the Spirit is seen in the worship, fellowship and witness of the Church here and now. But it carries a necessary reference to a greater future which is prayed for and expected. 'Do not be afraid; I am the first and the last, and the living one. I was dead, and see, I am alive forever and ever; and I have the keys of Death and of Hades' (Rev. 1.17–18). The image of the second coming of Christ signifies that God will be for us at the end, none other than who God has already been in the creation of the world and in the life, death and resurrection of Christ. The judge of the world will be none other than its saviour. The end of creation is Christ-shaped, as was its beginning. He is the one by whom and for whom all things were created. In this respect, the doctrine of the second coming cannot simply be discarded as a piece of quaint mythology which was obsolete after the dashing of first-century hopes for an early end of the world. It is integral to Christian

doctrine because of the eschatological and christological orienta-
tion of its doctrines of creation and redemption. If the creation
is centred on Jesus Christ from its foundation to its fulfilment,
we must expect God to be revealed in the form of Christ at the
end of time.[37] A non-literal interpretation of a return on the
clouds should not be allowed to obscure this central claim.

The new world which is already being created by God is not
another world, but the old world renewed. In this respect there
is both continuity and discontinuity between the sovereignty
which is now hidden and the sovereignty to be fully revealed.
The eschatological kingdom is not a regress to the Garden of
Eden, but a Holy City, a place of culture, society and embodied
life. It is, moreover, not merely a human habitat but a place for
the renewing of the whole of God's creation, an idea whose
power we should not underestimate. The philosopher F. H.
Bradley once remarked that when most people get to heaven
they will first go looking for their pet dog before they sing
with the angels.

Recent ecofeminist writing has drawn attention to two
features of eschatology which it regards as problematic. One
claim is that the discontinuity perceived between this world and
the next promotes the dangerous view that this world's ecosystem
is provisional only and therefore dispensable. This is a variation
on the Marxist theme that other-worldly concerns function as a
demobilizing ideology. They undermine one's best efforts to
improve the present by the false consolation of a better future
elsewhere. The link between Christian other-worldly eschatology
and environmental exploitation is now frequently made. 'Chris-
tendom is surely not accidentally the culture whose holy book
happens to culminate in a vision of the imminent devastation of
the earth, the culture that has developed the technologies and
politics capable of Armageddon, nuclear or greenhouse.'[38]

Allied to this criticism of traditional eschatology is the claim
that it is predicated upon a notion of divine sovereignty which
promotes relationships of power typically found in patriarchal attitudes. This criticism can be found both in Christian and in
post-Christian forms of ecofeminism. Thus Rosemary Radford
Ruether argues that apocalyptic imagery is based upon fantasy

and escapism. It seeks to evade death and thus the biosphere which we inhabit. This is founded upon a notion of God as unrelated to the earth, the body and mortality.[39] Sallie McFague argues that models of God are not to be judged by their correspondence to God's being but by their adequacy from the perspective of modern science, the interpretation of the Christian faith, our embodied experience and the well-being of the planet and its life-forms.[40] Preferring the model of God as the body of the world, she appears to argue in the final chapter of her recent book that Christian hope can only be for this world. An eschatological ideal is simply a heuristic device for tackling the problems and challenges of the present. The vision of the future serves as a goad and a goal which can assist us now in reforming this world. Her concluding reflections are brave but pessimistic. They echo Bertrand Russell's remarks about the need to meet life with an attitude of unyielding despair.

> The decay of our planet is probably inevitable, so we might as well just accept it. What real chance do we have of turning things around? All of this is probably true. Those who fought the plague in Albert Camus's novel by that name did not expect to exterminate the plague or even to escape it themselves. They only decided to live differently while they did live, to live as if life mattered while they had it, to live with integrity in light of the brutal reality that defined their world. One has to get up in the morning and look in the mirror. It may come to nothing more than that.[41]

The replacement of traditional images of divine transcendence and eschatological hope with pantheist models of divine presence is evident in much post-Christian ecofeminism. The image of God or the Goddess is one which symbolizes a whole of which we are a part. By drawing our attention to this whole the image of the divine both reminds us that we are deeply connected to all matter and also disabuses of the notion that we are the centre and masters of created reality. Thus Carol Christ, who has abandoned the Church for the Wicca movement, speaks of our being part of a whole which includes the earth, the sky, and all other forms of life. The divinity of which we are a part is the life, death and change we daily experience. There is no reality other than this.[42]

We see here what may be the most significant fault-line in contemporary Christian theology. Do traditional images of divine sovereignty, transcendence, action and eschatology liberate, empower, and command our allegiance? Or do these images tyrannize, dehumanize, infantilize and desensitize us to the issues and challenges of today? Closely related to this is the wider question of whether we can retain the central themes of theological realism which have traditionally included the ontological independence of God beyond the matter and mind of the world, divine action in creation and redemption, and the hope of resurrection and the life everlasting.

I have tried to argue that within the doctrine of creation there is a constellation of ideas which stand or fall together. These include the sovereignty of God as it is expressed in the Old Testament; the doctrine of creation out of nothing; the revealing of the Creator in covenant and incarnation; and the fulfilment of the Creator's intent in an eschatological reality. At the same time, I have tried to show that the contemporary exposition of these ideas must involve some readjustment through the conversation with modern cosmology, evolutionary biology and those who give sustained attention to the significance of the non-human creation. Yet I have attempted to show that concern with the contingency, worth and beauty of the creation everywhere can be married with faith in a sovereign creator and an incarnate saviour.

Belief in a transcendent creator and redeemer, coupled with hope in the world to come, need not be demobilizing notions which prevent us from active concern for the creation here and now. These may empower and liberate as effectively as any ideology. The example of the saints and martyrs of the Church bears witness to this.

In *The Belief in Progress* John Baillie once argued that history can only have a final meaning by virtue of divine action within and upon it. This divine action has a single centre in the history of Israel and Jesus, and it extends to all 'whose lives are determined by a positive relation to that centre'.[43] Christian faith is perpetually caught within a tension between prophetic and apocalyptic possibilities. On one side, it lives by the faith that with the resurrection of Christ and the descent of the Spirit a new way of life has become possible. On the other side, creation is beset by ills which cannot be relieved by any forward movement of history but only when that history has yielded to another kingdom. It is within this tension that the dynamics of the Christian life are found. Thus he writes, drawing on the insights of Reinhold Niebuhr:

> Christianity must always maintain a realized and a futurist eschatology in balance, if never in equipoise. In neglecting the latter it either shuts its eyes to the tragic realities of our continuing warfare or, alternatively, harbours utopian illusions of the possibility of their disappearance from the earthly scene. But in neglecting the former it is failing to understand the specific character, the promises and opportunities, of the years of grace.[44]

The realized and the future aspects of eschatology are interdependent, and this provides a response to those who see eschatology as enervating and debilitating. The prospect of the future is already anticipated in the present, and thus the latter is charged with hope, energy and expectation. Without that prospect the present is spiked with doubt, misgivings and loss of confidence. Hope for the creation is inseparably linked to hope in God the maker of heaven and earth, in Jesus Christ the incarnate Word, and in the Holy Spirit of life and love.

NOTES

1 Creation in the Bible

1 Gerhard von Rad, *Genesis*, London, SCM, 1961, p. 44. Von Rad's approach is analysed by H. H. Schmid, 'Creation, righteousness and salvation', in Bernhard Anderson (ed.) *Creation in the Old Testament*, London, SPCK, 1984, pp. 102–17.

2 Cf. Schmid, 'Creation, righteousness and salvation'.

3 Schmid, 'Creation, righteousness and salvation', p. 105.

4 R. Pettazzoni cited by Claus Westermann, *Genesis: An Introduction*, Minneapolis, Augsburg Fortress, 1992, p. 20. For a recent analysis of the Genesis story alongside other creation stories, see Ellen Van Wolde, *Stories of the Beginning*, London, SCM, 1996.

5 I am following here the exposition of Bernhard Anderson, *From Creation to New Creation*, Minneapolis, Augsburg Fortress, 1994, p. 24.

6 Angela Tilby, *Science and the Soul*, London, SPCK, 1992, p. 98.

7 Westermann, *Genesis: An Introduction*, pp. 26ff.

8 Anderson, *From Creation to New Creation*, p. 44.

9 Brevard Childs, *Biblical Theology of the Old and New Testaments*, London, SCM, 1992, p. 386.

10 Cf. Childs, *Biblical Theology*, pp. 407–8.

11 *New Jerome Bible Commentary*, London, Geoffrey Chapman, 1992, pp. 4–5.

12 'Attempts to date elements of Genesis 1—11 are at best plausible rather than probable, and involve circular arguments. This is not to say that it is wrong to try to date parts of Genesis 1—11, but rather that we should not allow such attempts to make us read the text superficially, as though we knew all that it has to say once we have assigned a date and setting. Even if we could be certain about dates and settings, we should still have to consider the following questions: how do the narratives function within the whole, and what interest do we, the readers, bring with us to the interpretation of Genesis 1—11?' John Rogerson, *Genesis 1—11*, Sheffield, Sheffield Academic Press, 1991, p. 77.

13 Hugh Miller, *The Testimony of the Rockes*, London, 1857, ch. 2. For discussion of the Christian reception of modern science in the nine-

teenth century, see Owen Chadwick, *The Victorian Church*, Part I, London, A. & C. Black, 1966, pp. 558–68; Andrew L. Drummond and James Bulloch, *The Church in Victorian Scotland 1843–1874*, Edinburgh, St Andrew Press, 1975, pp. 215–39.

14 Augustine, *Confessions*, Book XII, xiii. For a discussion of the interpretation of Genesis 1 in the history of the Church see Stanley L. Jaki, *Genesis 1 Through the Ages*, London, Thomas More Press, 1992. Jaki's thesis is that for much of the Church's history the interpretation of Genesis 1 has been skewed through misguided attempts to square its details with the prevailing scientific wisdom.

15 Augustine, *City of God*, Book XI, ch. 6.

16 Russell Stannard, *Science and Wonders: Conversations about Science and Belief* London, Faber & Faber, 1996, pp. xiii–xiv.

17 Scottish Office, *Curriculum and Assessment in Scotland, National Guidelines: Religious and Moral Education 5–15*, Edinburgh, Scottish Office Education Department, 1992, p.24.

18 Brevard Childs, *Introduction to the Old Testament as Scripture*, Philadelphia, Fortress, 1979, p. 150.

19 This argument is developed by Ted Peters in *Cosmos as Creation*, Nashville, Abingdon Press, 1989, pp. 45–114.

20 Cf. the discussion on preservation in Wolfhart Pannenberg, *Systematic Theology*, vol. II, Edinburgh, T. & T. Clark, 1994, p. 35.

21 Philo, *De Opificio Mundi*, trans. in *The Works of Philo*, Peabody, Mass., Henrikson, 1993, XXXIII (69), p. 10. I am indebted here to Francis Watson's *Text and Truth: Redefining Biblical Theology*, Edinburgh, T. & T. Clark, 1997, pp. 277ff.

22 Cf. Anderson, *From Creation to New Creation*, pp. 14f.

23 *Genesis*, p. 58.

24 Lynn White, 'The historical roots of our ecological crisis', *Science*, 155 (1967), pp. 1203–7.

25 *Genesis*, p. 58.

26 Anderson, *From Creation to New Creation*, p. 130.

27 This is impressively elaborated by Douglas John Hall, *Imaging God: Dominion as Stewardship*, Grand Rapids, Eerdmans, 1986.

28 Cf. Daniel Migliore, *Faith Seeking Understanding*, Grand Rapids, Eerdmans, 1991, pp. 82ff.

29 I am heavily indebted here to Rogerson, *Genesis 1—11*, pp. 19ff.

30 Cf. Rogerson, *Genesis 1—11*, pp.19ff.

31 Ruth Page, 'Theology and the ecological crisis', *Theology*, 99 (1996), p. 111. This is developed in her recent study *God and the Web of Creation*, London, SCM, 1996, Part Three.

32 I am following an account given by John Pick, *Gerard Manley Hopkins, Priest and Poet*, Oxford, Oxford University Press, 1942, pp. 31ff.

33 Walter Brueggemann, *Genesis*, Atlanta, John Knox, 1982, p. 36.

34 Cf. Childs, *Biblical Theology*, p. 391.

35 Alan Lewis, *Theatre of the Gospel*, Edinburgh, Handsel Press, 1984, pp. 26–7.

36 George MacLeod, *The Whole Earth Shall Cry Glory*, Iona, Wild Goose Publications, 1985, p. 8.

37 'God's Grandeur', *The Poems of Gerard Manley Hopkins*, eds. W. H. Gardner and N. H. MacKenzie, London, Oxford University Press, 1967, p. 66.

38 Cf. James Finn Cotter, *Inscape: The Christology and Poetry of Gerard Manley Hopkins*, Pittsburgh, University of Pittsburgh Press, 1972, pp. 167ff.

39 In what follows I am indebted to John Goldingay's discussion in *Theological Diversity and the Authority of the Old Testament*, Grand Rapids, Eerdmans, 1987, pp. 200–39.

40 Cf. William Johnstone, ' "The fear of the Lord is the beginning of wisdom": The biblical warrant for a university and much else besides', in Alan Main (ed.), *But Where Shall Wisdom be Found?*, Aberdeen, Aberdeen University Press, 1995, p. 27.

41 Karl Barth, *Church Dogmatics* III/1, Edinburgh, T. & T. Clark, 1958, p. 55.

42 *Church Dogmatics* III/1, p. 46.

43 *Church Dogmatics* III/1, p. 364.

44 Dietrich Bonhoeffer, *Letters and Papers from Prison*, London, SCM, 1953, p. 286.

2 Creation and Cosmology

1 Cf. Christopher Stead, *Philosophy in Christian Antiquity*, Cambridge, Cambridge University Press, 1994, pp. 67f.

2 Jostein Gaarder, *Sophie's World*, London, Phoenix House, 1995, p. 27.

3 *Timaeus*, 29D, 30A. Jaroslav Pelikan has argued that the Septuagintal translation of Genesis 1—2 was itself influenced by the *Timaeus*.

4 *First Apology* 59, *Ante-Nicene Fathers*, I, Grand Rapids, Eerdmans, 1981, p.183.

5 Richard Sorabji, *Time, Creation and the Continuum*, London, Duckworth, 1983, pp. 232ff.

6 Aristotle, *Physics*, I.7–8.

7 Gerhard May, *Creation out of Nothing*, Edinburgh, T. & T. Clark, 1994, pp. 156ff.

8 *Summa Contra Gentiles*, London, Burns, Oates & Washbourne, 1923, 2.38, pp.84–5. Cf. the extensive discussion in *Summa Theologiae*, 1ae.46.

9 May, *Creation out of Nothing*, pp. 177–8.

10 Jürgen Moltmann, *God in Creation*, London, SCM, 1985, p. 88.

11 Tertullian, *Against Hermogenes*, 15, *Ante-Nicene Fathers*, III, Grand Rapids, Eerdmans, 1951, p. 485.

12 Cf. Norbert M. Samuelson, *Judaism and the Doctrine of Creation*, Cambridge, Cambridge University Press, 1994, p.133. A. P. Hayman has suggested that Jewish reflection upon creation out of nothing may have largely been a response to developments within Islam and Christianity. 'The doctrine of creation in Sefer Yesira: some text-critical problems', in Gabrielle Sed-Rajna (ed.), *Rashi 1040–1990: Hommage à Ephraim E. Urbach*, Paris-Troyes, Congrès européen des Études juives, 1990, pp. 219–227.

13 Cf. Jacob Agus, *The Evolution of Jewish Thought*, New York, Abelard-Schuman, 1959, p. 187. Similar arguments concerning the God–world relationship are rehearsed by Alon Goshen-Gottschein, 'Creation', in A. A. Cohen and P. R. Mendes-Flohr (eds.), *Contemporary Jewish Religious Thought*, New York, Scribner's, 1987, pp. 114–18.

14 Thomas J. O'Shaughnessy, *Creation and the Teaching of the Qur'an*, Rome, Biblical Institute Press, 1985, p. 4.

15 Cited in W. Montgomery Watt (ed.), *Islamic Creeds: A Selection*, Edinburgh, Edinburgh University Press, 1994, p. 76. For a recent comparative study of the concepts of creation in Judaism, Christianity, Islam and Hinduism, see Keith Ward, *Religion and Creation*, Oxford, Clarendon, 1996.

16 Jaroslav Pelikan, *The Emergence of the Catholic Tradition*, Chicago, University of Chicago Press, 1971, p. 204.

17 In recent theology various attempts have been made to rectify this defect. Cf. Yves Congar, *I Believe in the Holy Spirit*, 3 vols., London, Geoffrey Chapman, 1983; Jürgen Moltmann, *The Spirit of Life*, London, SCM, 1992; Patrick Sherry, *Spirit and Beauty: An Introduction to Theological Aesthetics*, Oxford, Oxford University Press, 1992.

18 *De Spiritu Sancto*, XVI.38, trans. in *The Nicene and Post-Nicene Fathers*, Second Series, vol. VIII, Grand Rapids, Eerdmans, 1983, p.23.

19 T. F. Torrance, *The Trinitarian Faith*, Edinburgh, T. & T. Clark, 1988, pp. 76–109. Torrance is here following Karl Barth. 'In the same freedom and love in which God is not alone in Himself but is the eternal begetter of the Son, who is the eternally begotten of the

Father, He also turns as Creator *ad extra* in order that absolutely and outwardly He may not be alone but the One who loves in freedom.

... The eternal fellowship between Father and Son, or between God and His Word, thus finds a correspondence in the very different but not dissimilar fellowship between God and his creature.' Karl Barth, *Church Dogmatics* III/1, Edinburgh, T. & T. Clark, 1958, p. 50.

20 Paul Tillich, *Systematic Theology* vol. I, Chicago, University of Chicago Press, 1951, p.253.

21 David Pailin, *God and the Processes of Reality*, London, Routledge, 1989, p. 126.

22 Cf. D. W. D. Shaw, 'Process thought and creation', *Theology*, 78 (1975), pp. 346–55.

23 John B. Cobb and David R. Griffin, *Process Theology*, Philadelphia, Westminster Press, 1976, pp. 65 ff.

24 Moltmann, *God in Creation*, p. 79. A similar conflation of creation and preservation is present in Schleiermacher. Uneasy with the anthropomorphic connotations of creation out of nothing, Schleiermacher perceives the religious significance of the doctrine of creation in its expression of the absolute dependence of all things upon God. Friedrich Schleiermacher, *Christian Faith*, Edinburgh, T. & T. Clark, 1928, Section 41, pp. 152 ff.

25 Moltmann, *God in Creation*, pp. 84–5.

26 Wolfhart Pannenberg, *Systematic Theology*, vol. II, Edinburgh, T. & T. Clark, 1994, pp. 20 ff.

27 Eberhard Jüngel, *God as the Mystery of the World*, Edinburgh, T. & T. Clark, 1983, p. 384.

28 John Macmurray, *Freedom in the Modern World*, London, Faber & Faber, 1932, pp. 175 ff.

29 A similar criticism of recent ecological theology is developed by Bronislaw Szerszynski, 'The metaphysics of environmental concern: a critique of ecotheological antidualism', *Studies in Christian Ethics*, 6.2 (1993), pp. 67–78. Cf. Gillian McCulloch, 'An exploration of the deconstruction of dualism in theology', University of Aberdeen, Ph.D. thesis, 1996.

30 See the discussion in William Lane Craig, *The Cosmological Argument from Plato to Leibniz*, London, Macmillan, 1980.

31 Richard Swinburne, *Is There a God?*, Oxford, Oxford University Press, 1996, p. 68.

32 Norman Malcolm, *Ludwig Wittgenstein: A Memoir*, London, Oxford University Press, 1958, p. 70.

33 *Sunday Times*, Books Section, 4 February 1996, pp. 2–3.

34 I am following the popular exposition offered by Russell Stannard, *Doing Away with God? Creation and the Big Bang*, London, Marshall Pickering, 1993, ch. 1.

35 Ian Barbour, 'Religious responses to the big bang', in Clifford N. Matthews and Roy Abraham Varghese (eds.), *Cosmic Beginnings and Human Ends*, Chicago, Open Court, 1995, p. 381.

36 Angela Tilby, *Science and the Soul*, London, SPCK, 1992, p. 109.

37 Stephen Hawking, *A Brief History of Time*, London, Bantam, 1988, pp. 156–7.

38 I owe this to Ted Peters (ed.), *Cosmos as Creation: Theology and Science in Consonance*, Nashville, Abingdon, 1989, p. 54.

39 Stephen Hawking, *Black Holes and Baby Universes*, London, Bantam, 1993, p. 90. For further critical discussion of Hawking's position in relation to the Genesis creation account, see Michael Welker, 'Creation: big bang or the work of seven days?', *Theology Today*, 52 (1995/6), pp. 173–87.

40 E.g. Stannard, *Doing Away with God*, pp. 42ff; Keith Ward, *God, Chance and Necessity*, Oxford, Oneworld, 1996, p. 16.

41 Eric L. Mascall, *Christian Theology and Natural Science*, London, Longmans, Green & Co, 1956, p. 135. This point, however, is dependent upon a contrast between a timeless God and an everlasting world if God and the world are not to be rendered co-eternal as in process theology.

42 Peters, *Cosmos as Creation*, p. 59.

43 Quoted by David Kelsey in 'The doctrine of creation out of nothing' in E. McMullin (ed.), *Evolution and Creation*, Indiana, Notre Dame Press, 1985, p. 190.

44 For a criticism of the coherence of Hawking on imaginary time, quantum theory of gravity, and the spatialization of time, see William Lane Craig, '"What place, then, for a creator?" Hawking on God and creation' in *Theism, Atheism and Big Bang Cosmology*, Oxford, Clarendon, 1993, pp. 279–300.

45 'The temporality of God', in Robert John Russell, Nancey Murphy and C. J. Ishamm (eds.), *Quantum Cosmology and the Laws of Nature*, Vatican Observatory Foundation, 1993, p. 246.

46 *Confessions*, 13.12ff.

47 Lucas's position is developed in *The Future: An Essay on God, Temporality and Truth*, Oxford, Blackwell, 1989. For further discussion see Nelson Pike, *God and Timelessness*, New York, Schocken Books, 1970; Keith Ward, *Rational Theology and the Creativity of God*, Oxford, Blackwell, 1982.

3 Creation and Evolution

1 Annie Dillard, *Pilgrim at Tinker Creek*, London, Picador, 1976, pp. 125, 131.

2 John Brockman (ed.), *The Third Culture*, New York, Simon & Schuster, 1995.

3 These relationships are carefully assessed in John Hedley Brooke's *Science and Religion*, Cambridge, Cambridge University Press, 1991.

4 Charles Darwin, *Origin of Species*, Cambridge, Mass., Harvard University Press, 1964, pp. 471ff. Cf. the discussion in Brooke, *Science and Religion*, pp. 275ff.

5 Richard Dawkins, *The Blind Watchmaker*, Harmondsworth, Penguin, 1988, p. 40.

6 Cf. Brooke, *Science and Religion*, pp. 281f.

7 Cf. David Rosevear, *Creation Science*, Chichester, New Wine Press, 1991, p.158.

8 Eileen Barker, 'Scientific creationism', in John Durant (ed.), *Darwinism and Divinity: Essays on Evolution and Religious Belief*, Oxford, Blackwell, 1985, p. 193.

9 George M. Marsden, 'A case of the excluded middle', in Bellah and Greenspahn (eds.), *Uncivil Religion*, New York, Crossroad, 1987, p. 135. Hal Lindsey's *The Late Great Planet Earth* was the best-selling book in America during the 1970s.

10 Marsden, 'Excluded middle', p.139.

11 'Excluded middle', p.140.

12 The nearest to a standard creationist text is Henry Morris, *Scientific Creationism*, San Diego, Creation Life Publishers, 1974. Also highly influential is Duane Gish, *Evolution: The Fossils Say NO!*, San Diego, Creation Life Publishers, 1978.

13 Ussher's precise dating of creation was 9 am on 26 October 4004 BC.

14 Morris, *Scientific Creationism*, p. 38.

15 For a philosophical critique see Michael Ruse, *Darwinism Defended*, Reading, Mass., Addison & Wesley, 1982.

16 Michael R. Johnson, *Genesis, Geology and Catastrophism*, Exeter, Paternoster, 1988, p.40.

17 Johnson, *Genesis, Geology and Catastrophism*, p.33.

18 Morris, *Scientific Creationism*, p. 117.

19 For informed scientific rejoinder to creationism see also Laurie R. Godfrey (ed.), *Scientists Confront Creationism*, London, Norton & Co., 1984.

20 E.g. Langdon Gilkey, 'Creationism: the roots of the conflict', in R. M. Frye (ed.), *Is God a Creationist?*, New York, Scribner's, 1983, pp. 56–67.

21 Current disagreements amongst evolutionary theorists are apparent from the contributions to Brockman, *Third Culture*. Difficulties within current thinking are also set out by Phillip E. Johnston, *Darwin on Trial*, Downers Grove, IVP, 1991.

22 Niles Eldridge and Stephen Jay Gould, 'Punctuated equilibrium: an alternative to phyletic gradualism', in T. J. M. Schopf (ed.), *Models in Paleobiology*, San Francisco, Freeman, Cooper & Co., 1972, pp. 82–115.

23 E.g. Hugh Montefiore, *The Probability of God*, London, SCM, 1995, pp. 97ff.; Ward, *God, Chance and Necessity*, pp. 61ff.

24 Here I am indebted to A. R. Peacocke's *Creation and the World of Science*, Oxford, Oxford University Press, 1979, pp. 90ff. Peacocke's writings, however, suggest a more sanguine acceptance of determinacy within natural processes than is adopted in what follows.

25 Jacques Monod, *Chance and Necessity*, New York, Vintage Books, 1972, p. 44.

26 Monod, *Chance and Necessity*, p. 180.

27 *Blind Watchmaker*, pp. 316–18.

28 This type of response to Dawkins is developed by Richard Swinburne, *Is There A God?*, Oxford, Oxford University Press, 1996, pp. 58ff.

29 Cf. Hugh Montefiore, *Reclaiming the High Ground*, London, Macmillan, 1990, p. 88.

30 Freeman Dyson, *Disturbing the Universe*, New York, Harper & Row, 1979, p. 250. Cited by Ian G. Barbour, *Religion in an Age of Science*, London, SCM, 1990, p.136.

31 Thus Polkinghorne concludes that the contingent fruitfulness of the universe is a fact of interest calling for an explanation. John Polkinghorne, *Scientists as Theologians*, London, SPCK, 1996, p. 52.

32 For a critique of the hypothesis of multiple universes see John Leslie, *Universes*, London, Routledge, 1989, pp. 66–103.

33 Cf. Peacocke, *Creation and the World of Science*, pp. 116–17.

34 David Bartholomew, *God of Chance*, London, SCM, 1984.

35 In much of what follows I have borrowed from Barbour, *Religion in an Age of Science*.

36 This is argued for example by Arthur Peacocke, *God and Science: A Quest for Christian Credibility*, London, SCM, 1996, p. 16; and J. R. Lucas, *The Future: An Essay on God, Temporality and Truth*, Oxford, Blackwell, 1989, pp. 209ff.

37 For a valuable overview of the main options currently available in the

science–religion debate see Niels Henrik Gregersen, 'Three types of indeterminacy. On the difference between God's action in creation and in providence', in Niels H. Gregersen, Michael W. S. Parsons and Christoph Wassermann (eds.), *The Concept of Nature in Science and Theology*, Part I, Geneva, Labor et Fides, forthcoming, pp. 165–84.

38 John Polkinghorne, *Quarks, Chaos and Christianity*, London, Triangle, 1994, p. 43.

39 For a discussion of chaos theory and its theological implications see Robert John Russell, Nancey Murphy and Arthur R. Peacocke (eds.), *Chaos and Complexity*, Vatican Observatory Publications & Center for Theology and the Natural Sciences, Berkeley, 1995.

40 John Polkinghorne's most recent exposition of this approach can be found in 'Chaos theory and divine action', in W. Mark Richardson and Wesley J. Wildman (eds.), *Religion and Science: History, Method, Dialogue*, London, Routledge, 1996, pp. 243–52; and 'The Metaphysics of Divine Action', in Russell et al., *Chaos and Complexity*, pp. 147–56.

41 These themes are all explored by John Polkinghorne in *Science and Providence*, London, SPCK, 1989.

42 This aspect of the doctrine of preservation is developed by Hendrikus Berkhof, *Christian Faith*, Grand Rapids, Eerdmans, 1973, pp. 210ff.

43 This distinction between natural theology and the theology of nature is set out by Colin Gunton, *A Brief Theology of Revelation*, Edinburgh, T. & T. Clark, 1995, pp. 40–63.

44 For a moving attempt to integrate science and theology in this way see Ian Bradley, *The Power of Sacrifice*, London, Darton, Longman & Todd, 1994.

45 *Summa Theologiae* 2a2ae, Q64, art 1. Cf. Andrew Linzey, *Animal Theology*, London, SCM, 1994, pp. 12ff.

46 Keith Thomas, *Man and the Natural World: Changing Attitudes in England 1500–1800*, Harmondsworth, Penguin, 1984, pp. 18–19.

47 Thomas, *Man and the Natural World*, p. 22. Christopher Kaiser, however, has argued that the de-animation and mechanization of nature are not endemic to the Christian tradition. Biblical and patristic sources suggest that this was a later corruption of the doctrine of creation. *Creation and the History of Science*, London, Marshall Pickering, 1991.

48 Thomas, *Man and the Natural World*, p. 33.

49 *Man and the Natural World*, p. 139.

50 Linzey, *Animal Theology*, p. 135.

51 Peter Singer, 'All animals are equal', in Tom Regan and Peter Singer

(eds.), *Animal Rights and Human Obligations*, Englewood Cliffs, Prentice Hall, 1989, p. 79.

52 Cf. Alan White, 'Why animals cannot have rights', in Regan and Singer, *Animal Rights*, pp. 119ff.

53 'A trinitarian theology of the "chief end" of "all flesh"', in Charles Pinches and Jay B. McDaniel (eds.), *Good News for Animals? Christian Approaches to Animal Well-Being*, Maryknoll, Orbis, 1993, pp. 62–74.

54 For a sustained attack on humanocentric tendencies in the doctrine of creation see Ruth Page, *God and the Web of Creation*, London, SCM, 1996.

55 Text reproduced in Pinches and McDaniel, *Good News For Animals?*, p. 251.

56 Charles Birch, *A Purpose for Everything*, Connecticut, Twenty-Third Publications, 1990, p. 133.

57 This is argued by James Nash, *Loving Nature: Ecological Integrity and Christian Responsibility*, Nashville, Abingdon, 1991, pp. 179ff.

58 This is vigorously argued by Stephen Clark, *How to Think about the Earth*, London, Mowbray, 1993, pp. 106ff.

59 Barbour, *Religion in an Age of Science*, p. 147.

60 I am indebted here to the discussion in Barbour, *Religion in an Age of Science*, p. 190.

61 This is developed within a theological context by Philip Hefner, *The Human Factor: Evolution, Culture and Religion*, Minneapolis, Fortress Press, 1993, esp. pp. 23ff.

62 John Bowker, *Is God a Virus?*, London, SPCK, 1995, pp. 41–2.

63 Gerd Theissen, *Biblical Faith: An Evolutionary Approach*, Philadelphia, Fortress, 1985, pp. 112ff. Cf. Niels Gregersen, 'Theology in a Neo-Darwinian World', *Studia Theologica*, 48.2 (1994), pp. 146–7; Ward, *God, Chance and Necessity*, pp. 167–89.

64 Jürgen Moltmann, *The Way of Jesus Christ*, London, SCM, 1990, pp. 274ff.

4 Creation, Evil and the End of Life

1 David Hume, *Dialogues Concerning Natural Religion*, ed. R. H. Popkin, Indianapolis, Hackett, 1980, Part X, p. 63.

2 Augustine, *City of God*, XXII.22, London, Pelican Classics, 1972. For discussions of this aspect of Augustine's doctrine of evil see Elaine Pagels, *Adam, Eve and the Serpent*, New York, Random House, 1988, pp. 134ff.; G. R. Evans, *Augustine on Evil*, Cambridge, Cambridge University Press, 1982, ch. 4.

3 N. P. Williams, *The Ideas of the Fall and Original Sin*, London, Longmans, Green & Co, 1927, p. 215.

4 Cornelius Plantinga, *Not the Way It's Supposed to Be: A Breviary of Sin*, Grand Rapids, Eerdmans, 1995, p. 33.

5 Plantinga, *Not the Way It's Supposed to Be*, p. 37.

6 *Not the Way It's Supposed to Be*, p. 199.

7 John Polkinghorne, *Reason and Reality*, London, SPCK, 1991, p. 99.

8 The best survey of the history of theodicy remains John Hick, *Evil and the God of Love*, New York, Harper & Row, 1966. Ruth Page makes the important point that most traditional theodicies viewed the problem of evil only in human terms, as if animal suffering generated no theological issues. *God and the Web of Creation*, London, SCM, 1996, p. 94.

9 Richard Swinburne, *Is There a God?*, Oxford, Oxford University Press, 1996, p. 110.

10 Plotinus, *Enneads*, III.2.11, London, Faber & Faber, 1969, p. 170.

11 Fyodor Dostoevsky, *The Brothers Karamazov*, London, Heinemann, 1912, Book V, Chapter 4, p. 248.

12 William Styron, *Sophie's Choice*, London, Corgi Books, 1980, p. 642.

13 These points are clearly set out in Richard Bauckham 'Theodicy from Ivan Karamazov to Moltmann', *Modern Theology*, 4.1 (1987), pp. 83–97.

14 Emil Brunner, *The Christian Doctrine of Creation and Redemption*, London, Lutterworth, 1952, p. 20.

15 This is developed by John Polkinghorne from an evolutionary perspective, *Science and Christian Belief*, London, SPCK, 1994, pp. 84–5.

16 Simone Weil, *First and Last Notebooks*, London, Oxford University Press, 1970, p. 120.

17 This point is made by Stephen Davis in his edited symposium *Encountering Evil*, Edinburgh, T. & T. Clark, 1981. 'God is fully sovereign and omnipotent, but voluntarily shares some of his power with his creatures' (p. 127).

18 Cf. Robert Bernard Martin, *Gerard Manley Hopkins: A Very Private Life*, London, HarperCollins, 1991, p. 246.

19 This aspect of the theology in Hopkins' poetry is assessed by Paul Fiddes, *Freedom and Limit: A Dialogue Between Christian Literature and Doctrine*, London, Macmillan, 1991, pp. 128ff.

20 Fiddes, *Freedom and Limit*, p. 143.

21 'That Nature is a Heraclitean Fire and of the Comfort of the Resurrection', in W. H. Gardner and N. H. MacKenzie (eds.), *The Poems of Gerard Manley Hopkins*, London, Oxford University Press, 1967, pp. 105–6.

22 E.g. Paul Davies, *The Last Three Minutes*, London, Phoenix, 1994.

23 Cf. Polkinghorne's remark, 'This is why many of us find the tone of the writings of Teilhard de Chardin to be ultimately unhelpful.' *Science and Christian Belief*, p. 162.

24 'A free man's worship', in *Why I am not a Christian*, New York, Simon & Schuster, 1957, p. 107. This point is echoed by Steven Weinberg. 'The more the universe seems comprehensible, the more it also seems pointless. But if there is no solace in the fruits of research, there is at least some consolation in the research itself. . . . The effort to understand the universe is one of the very few things that lifts human life above the level of farce, and gives it some of the grace of tragedy.' *The First Three Minutes*, p.144; quoted by Ian G. Barbour, *Religion in an Age of Science*, London, SCM, 1990, p. 151.

25 'Theological Questions to Scientists', in A. R. Peacocke (ed.), *The Sciences and Theology in the Twentieth Century*, London, Oriel Press, 1981, pp. 14–15.

26 What follows is indebted to the discussion in Mark William Worthing, *God, Creation and Contemporary Physics*, Minneapolis, Augsburg Fortress, 1996, pp. 159–98.

27 Freeman Dyson, *Infinite in All Directions*, New York, Harper & Row, 1988, pp. 97ff.

28 Dyson, *Infinite in All Directions*, p. 107.

29 *Infinite in All Directions*, p. 111.

30 Frank Tipler, *The Physics of Immortality*, London, Macmillan, 1995, p. xv.

31 Tipler, *The Physics of Immortality*, pp. 221ff.

32 *The Physics of Immortality*, pp. 218, 220.

33 Davies, *The Last Three Minutes*, p. 126.

34 Fergus Kerr, *Theology After Wittgenstein*, Oxford, Blackwell, 1986, p. 186.

35 *Science and Christian Belief*, p. 165.

36 Keith Ward, *Rational Theology and the Creativity of God*, Oxford, Blackwell, 1982, p. 202.

37 This is elaborated by Jürgen Moltmann in *The Way of Jesus Christ*, London, SCM, 1990, pp. 313ff.

38 Catherine Keller, 'Eschatology, ecology and a green ecumenacy', in Rebecca Chopp and Mark Lewis Taylor (eds.), *Reconstructing Christian Theology*, Minneapolis, Fortress, 1994, p. 341.

39 Rosemary Radford Ruether, *Gaia and God: An Ecofeminist Theology of Earth Healing*, London, SCM, 1993, p. 83.

40 Sallie McFague, *The Body of God: An Ecological Theology*, London, SCM, 1993, p. 152.
41 McFague, *The Body of God*, p. 208.
42 Carol Christ, 'Rethinking theology and nature', in Irene Diamond and Gloria Feman Orenstein (eds.), *Reweaving the World: The Emergence of Ecofeminism*, San Francisco, Sierra Club Books, 1990, pp. 65–6.
43 John Baillie, *The Belief in Progress*, Oxford, Oxford University Press, 1950, p. 189.
44 Baillie, *Belief in Progress*, p. 207.

SELECT BIBLIOGRAPHY

Anderson, Bernhard, *From Creation to New Creation*. Minneapolis, Augsburg Fortress, 1992

Barbour, Ian, *Religion in an Age of Science*. London, SCM, 1990

Barth, Karl, *Church Dogmatics* III/1. Edinburgh, T. & T. Clark, 1958

Brooke, John Hedley, *Science and Religion*. Cambridge, Cambridge University Press, 1991

Craig, William Lane, *The Cosmological Argument from Plato to Leibniz*. London, Macmillan, 1980

Craig, William Lane (ed.), *Theism, Atheism and Big Bang Cosmology*. Oxford, Clarendon, 1993

Davis, Stephen (ed.), *Encountering Evil*. Edinburgh, T. & T. Clark, 1981

Dawkins, Richard, *The Blind Watchmaker*. Harmondsworth, Penguin, 1988

Frye R. M. (ed.), *Is God a Creationist?*. New York, Scribner's, 1993

Hall, Douglas J., *Imaging God: Dominion as Stewardship*. Grand Rapids, Eerdmans, 1986

Hefner, Philip, *The Human Factor: Evolution, Culture and Religion*. Minneapolis, Fortress, 1993

Hick, John, *Evil and the God of Love*. New York, Harper & Row, 1966

Kaiser, Christopher, *Creation and the History of Science*. London, Marshall Pickering, 1991

Linzey, Andrew, *Animal Theology*. London, SCM, 1994

May, Gerhard, *Creation out of Nothing*. Edinburgh, T. & T. Clark, 1994

McFague, Sallie, *The Body of God: An Ecological Theology*. London, SCM, 1993

Moltmann, Jürgen, *God in Creation*. London, SCM, 1985

Moltmann, Jürgen, *The Way of Jesus Christ*. London, SCM, 1990

Nash, James, *Loving Nature: Ecological Integrity and Christian Responsibility*. Nashville, Abingdon, 1991

Page, Ruth, *God and the Web of Creation*. London, SCM, 1996

Pannenberg, Wolfhart, *Systematic Theology*, vol. II. Edinburgh, T. & T. Clark, 1994

Peacocke, A. R. *Creation and the World of Science*. Oxford, Oxford University Press, 1979

Peters, Ted (ed.), *Cosmos as Creation*. Nashville, Abingdon, 1989

Pinches, Charles, and McDaniel, Jay B. (eds.), *Good News for Animals? Christian Approaches to Animal Well-Being*. Maryknoll, Orbis, 1993

Plantinga, Cornelius, *Not the Way It's Supposed to Be: A Breviary of Sin*. Grand Rapids, Eerdmans, 1995

Polkinghorne, John, *Quarks, Chaos and Christianity*. London, Triangle, 1994

Polkinghorne, John, *Science and Creation: The Search for Understanding*. London, SPCK, 1988

Rogerson, John, *Genesis 1—11*. Sheffield, Sheffield Academic Press, 1991

Ruether, Rosemary Radford, *Gaia and God: An Ecofeminist Theology of Earth Healing*. London, SCM, 1993

Stannard, Russell, *Science and Wonders: Conversation about Science and Belief*. London, Faber & Faber, 1996

Swinburne, Richard, *Is There a God?* Oxford, Oxford University Press, 1996

Thomas, Keith, *Man and the Natural World: Changing Attitudes in England 1500–1800*. Harmondsworth, Penguin, 1984

Tilby, Angela, *Science and the Soul*. London, SPCK, 1992

Tipler, Frank, *The Physics of Immortality*. London, Macmillan, 1995

Torrance, Thomas F., *The Trinitarian Faith*. Edinburgh, T. & T. Clark, 1988

Ward, Keith, *God, Chance and Necessity*. Oxford, Oneworld, 1996

Ward, Keith, *Religion and Creation*. Oxford, Clarendon, 1996

Westermann, Claus, *Genesis: An Introduction*. Minneapolis, Augsburg Fortress, 1992

Worthing, Mark William, *God, Creation and Contemporary Physics*. Minneapolis, Augsburg Fortress, 1996

Index

The Society for Promoting Christian Knowledge (SPCK) has as its purpose three main tasks:

- **Communicating the Christian faith in its rich diversity**
- **Helping people to understand the Christian faith and to develop their personal faith**
- **Equipping Christians for mission and ministry**

SPCK Worldwide serves the Church through Christian literature and communication projects in over 100 countries. Special schemes also provide books for those training for ministry in many parts of the developing world. SPCK Worldwide's ministry involves Churches of many traditions. This worldwide service depends upon the generosity of others and all gifts are spent wholly on ministry programmes, without deductions.

SPCK Bookshops support the life of the Christian community by making available a full range of Christian literature and other resources, and by providing support to bookstalls and book agents throughout the UK. SPCK Bookshops' mail order department meets the needs of overseas customers and those unable to have access to local bookshops.

SPCK Publishing produces Christian books and resources, covering a wide range of inspirational, pastoral, practical and academic subjects. Authors are drawn from many different Christian traditions, and publications aim to meet the needs of a wide variety of readers in the UK and throughout the world.

The Society does not necessarily endorse the individual views contained in its publications, but hopes they stimulate readers to think about and further develop their Christian faith.

For further information about the Society, please write to:
SPCK, Holy Trinity Church, Marylebone Road,
London NW1 4DU, United Kingdom.
Telephone: 0171 387 5282